# Watton through the ages

### by

### George Jessup

## MEMORIAL EDITION

# Watton through the ages

## by
## George Jessup

*Cover illustration of St. Mary's Church and portrait of George Jessup by Kevin Robinson*

This edition © 2003 J C Books
First printed 1985

ISBN 0 900616 69 5

Printed and published by Geo. R. Reeve Ltd., 9-11 Town Green, Wymondham, Norfolk.
Distributed by J C Books, 55 High Street, Watton, Norfolk, IP25 6AB.
Further copies may be obtained from the distributor. Tel: 01953 883488.

# Contents

Preface . . . . . . . . . . . . . . . . . . . . . . . . . . . . . . . . . . . . . . . . . . . . . . . . 5
Introduction . . . . . . . . . . . . . . . . . . . . . . . . . . . . . . . . . . . . . . . . . . . 7
"Watton Through The Ages" . . . . . . . . . . . . . . . . . . . . . . . . . . . . 8
St. Mary's Church . . . . . . . . . . . . . . . . . . . . . . . . . . . . . . . . . . . . . 17
The Congregational Chapel . . . . . . . . . . . . . . . . . . . . . . . . . . . . . 20
The Wesleyan Chapel . . . . . . . . . . . . . . . . . . . . . . . . . . . . . . . . . . 22
The Methodist Chapel . . . . . . . . . . . . . . . . . . . . . . . . . . . . . . . . . 22
The Poor of the Parish . . . . . . . . . . . . . . . . . . . . . . . . . . . . . . . . . 25
The Alms Houses . . . . . . . . . . . . . . . . . . . . . . . . . . . . . . . . . . . . . 28
Willow House . . . . . . . . . . . . . . . . . . . . . . . . . . . . . . . . . . . . . . . . 29
Harvey House . . . . . . . . . . . . . . . . . . . . . . . . . . . . . . . . . . . . . . . . 31
Public Services . . . . . . . . . . . . . . . . . . . . . . . . . . . . . . . . . . . . . . . 33
The Railway . . . . . . . . . . . . . . . . . . . . . . . . . . . . . . . . . . . . . . . . . 41
Loch Neaton . . . . . . . . . . . . . . . . . . . . . . . . . . . . . . . . . . . . . . . . . 44
Education . . . . . . . . . . . . . . . . . . . . . . . . . . . . . . . . . . . . . . . . . . . . 51
Crown Hotel . . . . . . . . . . . . . . . . . . . . . . . . . . . . . . . . . . . . . . . . . 56
Wayland Hall . . . . . . . . . . . . . . . . . . . . . . . . . . . . . . . . . . . . . . . . 60
The Watton Almanack and Advertising Medium of 1891 . . . . . 62
The Wayland Show . . . . . . . . . . . . . . . . . . . . . . . . . . . . . . . . . . . . 72
The Markets . . . . . . . . . . . . . . . . . . . . . . . . . . . . . . . . . . . . . . . . . 77
"In Wayland Woods the Babes were Found" . . . . . . . . . . . . . . . 80
The Band . . . . . . . . . . . . . . . . . . . . . . . . . . . . . . . . . . . . . . . . . . . . 83
The Cottage Hospital . . . . . . . . . . . . . . . . . . . . . . . . . . . . . . . . . . 84
The R.A.F. Station . . . . . . . . . . . . . . . . . . . . . . . . . . . . . . . . . . . . 88
The Queen's Hall . . . . . . . . . . . . . . . . . . . . . . . . . . . . . . . . . . . . . 93
Watton Memorial Playing Field . . . . . . . . . . . . . . . . . . . . . . . . . 94
Watton Sports Centre . . . . . . . . . . . . . . . . . . . . . . . . . . . . . . . . . . 97
Sport . . . . . . . . . . . . . . . . . . . . . . . . . . . . . . . . . . . . . . . . . . . . . . . . 98
The Cinemas . . . . . . . . . . . . . . . . . . . . . . . . . . . . . . . . . . . . . . . . . 110
The Red Cross Detachment . . . . . . . . . . . . . . . . . . . . . . . . . . . . . 112
St. John Ambulance Brigade . . . . . . . . . . . . . . . . . . . . . . . . . . . . 113
The Care of the Elderly . . . . . . . . . . . . . . . . . . . . . . . . . . . . . . . . 115
Changes Along the High Street . . . . . . . . . . . . . . . . . . . . . . . . . . 116
Changes Around the Town . . . . . . . . . . . . . . . . . . . . . . . . . . . . . . 122
A Few Schoolboy Memories . . . . . . . . . . . . . . . . . . . . . . . . . . . . 131
Miscellaneous . . . . . . . . . . . . . . . . . . . . . . . . . . . . . . . . . . . . . . . . 136
"In Conclusion" . . . . . . . . . . . . . . . . . . . . . . . . . . . . . . . . . . . . . . 149

# PREFACE

The seeds for this book were sown in the winter of 1971. After showing my illustrated programme of "Breckland Through the Ages" to a small group of friends, I concluded by putting on a few slides of "Old Watton".

This gave George Adcock the idea that we should collect as many old photographs of the town as we could and reproduce them into slides to make an illustrated programme of "Watton Through the Ages". A letter in the Thetford & Watton Times appealing for the loan of any interesting photographs of Watton brought an overwhelming response, some even being received from Canada.

It took 16 months of my spare time to sort out, reproduce the best, and compile the programme. Finally, the first showing was given on March 20th 1973. 450 tickets were sold within a fortnight and with so many people being disappointed in being unable to obtain one, the programme was repeated six months later. It has now been shown five times with all the proceeds going to local charities.

Many people who saw it, suggested that I should put it into book form and this I decided I would do when I retired. But then I found that writing articles, lecturing, leading nature excursions, giving commentaries to coach parties and maintaining a large garden, took up all my time. However, I decided to start writing the book last autumn, after having to give up gardening.

Every effort has been made to ensure the accuracy of the dates and other information, but in some cases different dates are shown for various events in old publications, the Great Fire of Watton being one of them. I had always read that this occurred on Saturday 25th April 1673, but when researching I came across a statement saying this date was incorrect and that the year was 1674.

A donation from each copy sold will go to the Loch Neaton project funds, at the request of George Jessup's family, to further his work.

I would like to thank everyone who has helped me in any way to produce this book, especially the staff of Watton Library, Norwich Central Library, Colman Rye Library, Norfolk Record Office, Eastern Counties Newspapers, Rev. P. Harrison, Watton Town Clerk, the businessmen who gave information about their firm's history in answer to my appeal in the two local papers and to Patrick Julnes for allowing a few extracts to be used from the "Watton Almanack" of 1891 that he discovered when modernising William Kendall's former shop.

Also, I would like to thank everyone for the loan of photographs, including Wiley Noble in America for risking sending a few of his treasured collection, taken during the American Air Forces stay at Watton during the war. I am sorry that there was insufficient space to print them all. Hopefully, one day, I shall be able to follow this book with one of "Watton Through the Years in Pictures", so save all your old Watton photographs.


George Jessup,
Watton, Norfolk. 1985.

# INTRODUCTION

The author comes from a long line of Country People intensely interested in their surroundings. Through this excellent book Mr. Jessup makes us aware how the needs of the local inhabitants have been met by each generation. Space does not allow mention of all the sources of information drawn on, or the people who have contributed so much to make Watton what it is today. Mr. Jessup is also well known for his illustrated talks on natural history and local topics. Watton has always had a sturdy independence and been prepared to work for what it needs. It surprises me that a town with such a small population as it was in 1920-1930 could support three large shops virtually selling the same goods.

The post war years saw rapid changes, depression and hard times. Now the many housing estates cater for a much larger population and factory units create employment. The period covered has seen many changes, not all for the better. The book will have a wide appeal, not only to residents, but also to those living in the locality.

R.G. Durrant,
High Street,
WATTON.

Please note that this book was originally published in 1985 and that many changes have taken place since.

# "WATTON THROUGH THE AGES"

Watton is an old market town that in the Domesday Book was described as Wadetuna, the town of the ford, from the Anglo-Saxon-WADAN. The area of the parish covers 1,808 acres and in addition to arable and meadow, there were large areas of woodland with Wayland Wood probably considerably larger than it is today.

The Church is the oldest building in the town and was founded in the reign of Henry I on land given to the Prior of Thetford by the Fitzwalter family. Its present position is inconvenient for the majority of the inhabitants, but when first built it was in a central position for the various hamlets of the parish. Near the church is the site of the old Manor House of which no trace remains above ground, but parts of what were thought to be its foundations have been unearthed at various times in a field adjacent.

The earliest historical records of Watton are associated with its market and in 1202 John de Vaux, who held Watton Hall Manor was granted a Market Charter by King John whereby a market could be held in the town every Friday, but in 1204 an enquiry was made under a writ as to whether the market here was not prejudicial to the market at Saham Toney, the adjoining parish, and it being found this was so, the charter authorising the holding of the market was recalled. Before the year was out however, the Manor had been conveyed by John de Vaux to his brother Oliver, who had a considerable influence with the King, and he thus obtained a new Charter by which the market was to be held every Wednesday, as it still is to day. At this time Saham Toney was a Royal Manor and much larger and wealthier than Watton, so it is understandable that the establishment of Watton market was resented at Saham. In 1375 friction between the two communities became so great that it developed into open violence. But for Watton the establishment of the market was crucial, both for the town's economic importance and also to the evolution of its physical shape. As the market place became the focus of the community, the town gradually developed around it and steadily spread westwards along what is now the High Street. At this time Neaton and Watton Green were entirely separate hamlets, each consisting of a small number of buildings grouped around the edge of the common grazing land.

In 1349 the Black Death accounted for many of Watton's inhabitants and of the thirty-two burials recorded in 1712, no less than twenty one of them succumbed to smallpox.

There is little documentary evidence of the history of the town prior to the 16th century, but from time to time excavations have revealed considerable evidence that the town was occupied by the Romans, and some archaeologists believe that Norwich Road and the High Street follow the line of a former Roman road.

*The High Street, 1972*

The "Old Town Book" of Watton records some quant items as to the life in the town. Some of the earliest of which refer to the various public feasts held annually on "Wisson Monday" and known as "Drynkyns". At these, there appears to have been a considerable consumption of food as well as drink, as shown by the "Bill of Fare" for the Drynkyn held in 1560 and included: — Paid for apples 10d., paid for 5 skore and four white herrings 2s. 4d., paid for 3½ lbs. raisins 5d., anny seeds 1d., a pint of honey 5d., two pints of "boter" 7d., ounce of pepper 3d., paid to Aldean's wife for dozen bread 1s., paid to France's wife for dozen cakes 1s., and various bakins 5s. A firkin of beer 1s. 3d., half a barrel of beer 2s. 6d. It appears that the Churchwardens and their wives were responsible for the catering on these occasions, but other people helped in providing the necessary food and drink. Collections were made to defray expenses and the balance went towards benefiting the poor, through the Churchwarden's accounts. In 1565 the balance for the poor was 14s. 6d and in 1566 it was 13s 10d.

*Brockbank's Baker's & Confectioners Shop - "George Hotel" (now Lloyd's Bank) - Durrant's Shop.*

There are a great many other interesting items in the "Old Town Book", a few of which are:—

1561 Paid to Browster for mending ye Bardrych of ye bells Vld.

1597 Henry Turner, James Hansard, Robert Breett, Nycolas Cock, and Henry Firket were chosen by the inhabitance of the towne of Watton for laying the towne for nayfull verme and fowles.

1587 George Hayward is appoynted to look to the bells for one whole yere, he shalll have for his laboure I shilling.

1592 November 17th. Bought of Thomas Skeene, the greate belle wheel, and he is to make it new agayn if it break in fyve yeres after at his own coste and charge; for it he is payd V shillings.

1600 "Hugh Turner, clark and vicar of Watton, and Dorothy Dunn of Hingham, a widow, were married on July 10th.

1603 It is recorded that Christopher Hey delivered to Humphrey Mosse and James Brat, I corslet, I pick, a sword, 2 daggers, I girdle, I headpiece with a cote and all things to it belonging. Prior to this there is an entry that £7. 8s. was paid from the Church funds for "A sword skabberk, a daggerd and a payn hanger". The purpose of supplying this warlike equipment is unknown, but possibly the two men thus equipped were the policemen of the day.

1659 Put out the bells keeping, and to keepe out the dogges of the Church and to awake all sleepers wch sleepe in divine service, to old

William Mayes for one whole yeare insueing 10/- per annum—2/6 to be payd every quarter by the Churchwardens.

1729 The "Terrier" of 1729 records: — "One pulpit cloth and cushion of purple with a good fringe; the former finely embroidered with silver and ye letters I.H.S., and ye date of ye yeare, given by good Mr. Scott, wch cost him eight guineas".

*Back of "George Hotel", Norwich to London stage coaches changed horses here, picture circa 1870.*

In the 16th and 17th centuries there were many records of the catholic sympathy shown by the good folk of Watton to those in trouble in other parts of the country and in 1666 £2. 12. 0 was given for the relief of the poor in the Great Fire of London. In May 1677 15s. 6d. was given for those who suffered in the dreadful fire at Northampton and similar donations were sent to many other places that suffered from fire, hail storms, gales and floods.

By the time Elizabeth I ascended the throne Watton was already the proud possessor of a Market Cross which was supported by eight oak pillars. Between two of them, on the south side, were placed the stocks and immediately above them was the Town's name, carved in Oak, "A Hare and a TUN". The Cross was taken down in 1820 and replaced by a "Stone Obelisk" marked with the distance to the neighbouring market towns.

The Cross was situated in the Market Square which at that time was considerably larger than the small area in front of the Wayland Hall, known as the Market Place to-day. Here the stall holders gathered each Wednesday including dealers in cloth, a considerable variety of woollen goods, fish, meat, vegetables and gloves, the latter were usually made of wool, with pigs skin much used as an alternative. The breeches worn by many of the male population were also made of pigs skin.

During Elizabeth's reign 1558-1603 a number of inns had been built near the town centre and the famous "George Coaching Hotel" which occupied the site of the present Lloyd's Bank, was already in existence. During the coaching era the Norwich to London Stage Coach changed horses at the George Hotel and the Holt to Thetford Coach also picked up passengers here. Other Inns situated near the Market Place included the "Angel", "Christopher", "Swann", "Griffin", and the "Bull", but not the present "Bull Hotel", although this earlier inn probably stood on the same site.

A number of crafts, trades and businesses flourished in Watton during the 16th and 17th century including, butchers, bakers, brewers, shoemakers, blacksmiths, wheelwrights, saddlers and coopers. But by far the most important industry was the manufacture of woollen cloth and the most influential men were the mercers who dealt in this business. One of the most prosperous of them was Christopher Hey who built the town's most distinctive landmark, the Clock Tower. The only known trade token for the town was issued by him. On one side it had his name and the Mercer's Arms and on the other side was the inscription "of Watton, Mercer C. M. H." Many of the mercers and some of the craftsmen were also landowners and farmers and some of their farm buildings were situated within a hundred yards or so of the Market Cross and agriculture was thus the main employer of labour.

With just over 400 people in the 17th century Watton was a small market town compared to the nearby market towns of Hingham and Swaffham. Judging by the fine houses still to be seen in the centre of both these places, it would appear that they had more prosperous families than Watton at this time. Besides the woollen industry at this period, Watton was also a celebrated "Butter Mart", great quantities of which were sent from the town to Downham Bridge, from whence the factors forwarded it to London by water.

On Saturday, April 25th 1674, a fire of terrible extent occurred in the town. Over sixty houses, the Butchers Shambles and other property were burnt down, the value of the destroyed property being estimated at £7,450, in addition to which goods to the value of £2,660 were consumed in the fire. A brief was granted the town to gather over all England until September 20th 1675. There was a good response to the appeal and rebuilding started quickly and in 1681 Thomas Baskerville visited Watton and described it as a small town, lately burnt, but now rebuilt, in which there is little remarkable save a fine new bowling green at the "George", where we dined.

*Town Pump, Clock Tower and Vincent's Chemist Shop, about 1914, note the water trough for cattle on edge of road, also the Street gas lamp.*

From the 16th century five annual fairs were held, on July 10th, October 11th and November 8th for cattle, on the first Wednesday of July for "stock" and on the second Wednesday of October for sheep.

On the north side of the town centre stands the Clock Tower built in 1679 by Christopher Hey. It has some ornamental battlements and an ornate cupola in which was placed a bell, known as the "Ting-Tang", to warn the inhabitants should fire break out again. The building also serves as a memorial to the "Great Fire" of Watton. Above the cupola is the town's coat of arms in the form of a barrel, also known as a "ton" and a hare, known in the country as a "wat", hence the name Watton. The original construction was of soft red bricks, but these were cement rendered about 1827 when a new clock, given to the town by Edward Stevens was inserted. At the same time a strip of wood from the old Market Cross was let into the face of the building.

The bottom part of the tower was once a "Lock-up" and has two strong studded doors. The clock was given a new luminous face in 1935 to commemorate the Silver Jubilee of King George V and Queen Mary.

Following the Proclamation of King George II on 29th June 1727, the then correspondent of the Norwich Mercury wrote that the inhabitants of Watton knew how to take advantage of every occasion for rejoicing. "Yesterday being appointed for Proclaiming our most gracious King, the morning was spent in adorning the Streets with Boughs and Garlands and the Houses with Tapestry and Pictures. At 3 p.m. a procession led by Mr. Reuben Muston the Sheriff, proceeded with Drums, Trumpets and other Musick. A mile from the town we met Thomas de Grey, Esq., our Truly Worthy Representative for the County. Next to the Sheriff went several Coaches, then the Town Sergeants with their fine Halberts, the Constables with Silk Streamers upon their staves, the Clergy in two Ranks, the Gentlemen and Country-men with above 300 horses and a vast number on foot, with a continual Acclaimation of Long Live King George II. In this order, with great Decency, we marched to the Cross and proclaimed his Majesty, upon which the shouts were the loudest ever heard in so small a town. We then proceeded into Cross Street and there the Gentlemen on horseback drank the King's health and treated the Ladies and the better sort of Countrymen with Wine, and gave a Barrel of Strong Beer to the Populace in the Street. Then the Gentlemen waited upon our Representative to the "George", where they drank the health of the King, the Queen and the rest of the Royal Family. The Evening was finely illuminated and hardly one house missed and a large Bonfire was made and another Barrel of Strong Beer given to the Populace. The festivities lasted until midnight, with the Bells Ringing without ceasing the whole time".

*The "Brewery House", now the "Chocolate Box". It was from an upstairs window that Mr. Frost threw the hot pennies on Valentine's Day.*

For several centuries the nation's prosperity relied heavily upon the wool trade but when it started to decline, agricultural areas like Watton had to adjust to other aspects of the industry. Hence more cereal crops were grown, dairy farming increased and the various fodder crops to support it were cultivated in increasing amounts.

From the mid 19th century there was a steady decline in agriculture locally and the National Census of 1851 showed that the farms around the town employed 119 agricultural workers, but twenty years later this figure had dropped to 87.

Apart from agriculture and its allied occupations there was no industry in Watton employing more than a few men until the coming of the brewery in 1809, but it was not until 1838 when Robert Stevens increased it's capacity that many people were thus employed.

With the advent of the railway, Tyrrell and Byfords and Julnes's set up their corn, coal and cattle food business by the railway sidings, as also did a half dozen coal merchants, and between them all about 80 workers were employed here until the railway was closed in 1964. Tyrrell and Byfords also started to manufacture cattle pellets etc., in two ex-R.A.F. Hangars on the Norwich Road in 1954, employing a staff of about 30.

From 1892, when Jacobs sold his horse breeding business, there do not appear to have been any new ventures providing employment for more than a few men until the Watton Sawmills were founded around 1913 and for the next fifteen years they were by far the largest employers of labour in the town.

By the early 1920's many workers began to find employment with the local building firms and both Tennants and Peeke-Vouts had a workforce of about 90 at their peak.

From 1936 when a start was made in building the R.A.F. Station until it was run down in 1969 more civilian workers were employed on the station than anywhere else and their peak figure was over 400.

Local Government changes became effective on April 1st 1974, when the Parish Council became the Town Council with a Town Mayor as its Chairman. Since that date the following townsfolk have held the Office of Town Mayor:—1974/75 and 1975/76 Mr. C. Mitchell, 1976/77 Mr. R. Thornhill, 1977/78 Mr. P. Rudling, 1978/79 Dr. P. D. Shanks, 1979/80 Mr. C. Cadman, 1980/81 Mr. O. Adcock, 1981/82 Mr. N. Eldridge, 1982/83 Mrs. J. Crabtree, 1983/84 Mr. T. Turley, 1984/85 Mr. C. Rudkin, 1985/86 Mr. C. Cadman. From the first elected members to Watton Parish Council in 1895 to the last elected in 1973, the council had the remarkable record of having only 3 Clerks and making this even more remarkable is that they all belonged to one family as follows:— 1895 to 1927 Mr. E. Harvey, 1927 to 1948 Mr. F. A. Harvey and 1948 to 1974 Mr. W. F. Harvey.

*Threshing at Jeremiah Jessup's, Redhill Nursery Farm, Watton, about 1898.*

# ST. MARY'S CHURCH

In the Domesday Book, compiled in 1086, it is stated that Watton had a church, but there don't appear to be any records as to where it was situated, or the date that it was built. However, it is most likely to have been on the same site as our present St. Mary's. It is generally accepted that this was built between 1100 and 1135 and is therefore the oldest building in the town. Of flint construction in the Norman and Gothic styles, it was originally dedicated to St. Giles, but was rededicated to St. Mary in the early 15th century. Its tower is round at the base, with an octagon belfry containing six bells. These were installed in 1899 owing to the introduction of Change Ringing in the 17th century which led to the wholesale recasting of all bells to make them into "peals" — a set of bells attuned to each other. Previously there were only three bells housed in a wooden spire and inscribed "John Brend made me in "1656-1658". The new bells were bought by public subscription at a cost of £300 and they carry the following inscription:—

1.  (Treble) This bell was given by members of the Watton Church Council.
2.  To the honour and glory of God. This peak of six bells was placed in St. Mary's Church, Watton, 1899 (MDCCCXCIX).
3.  For mercies undeserved this peal is raised; And may Thy Name, 0 God, through Christ be praised.
4.  Let Christ be known around, And loved whe'er we sound.
5.  With loving voice I call to Church and Prayer, And bid the living for the grave prepare.
6.  (Tenor) Praise God in His Sanctuary, Praise Him in the firmament of His Power.

Due to the rapid growth of the population in the early nineteenth century the north and south aisles of the church were taken down in 1840 to enable them to be extended in width, thus increasing the seating capacity from 260 to 480. This alteration made St. Mary's the only church in Norfolk that is wider than its length. To help defray the expenses of this alteration, the decorated font was sold to Ovington Church and replaced with the present one of Caen Stone with an oak cover. In 1852 the gallery in the church was removed, the floor lowered, an oak screen, pulpit and lectern erected, while in 1858 the church was closed for some weeks while further alterations were carried out. It was reopened on 16th June and the Norfolk Chronicle of 3rd July stated, "Very much has been done towards making our church more adapted for the worship of the Most High and it is most satisfactory to see the endeavours of the Vicar so ably seconded, not only by his parishioners, but by the neighbouring clergy and gentry. It is a most cheering sight in these days that a more earnest spirit really exists amongst nearly all classes".

*St. Mary's Church Sunday School outing about 1918*

One of the church's most treasured possessions is the curious wooden poor box, which represents the figure of a priest on whose chest is inscribed the words, "Remember the Poore, 1639". He is shown holding a bag with an orifice at the top where money can be placed before passing into the box below.

*Carved Wooden Poor Box.*
*in St. Mary's Church*

*Carving on the Market Cross,*
*demolished in 1820.*

There are several stained glass windows in the church and the one at the extreme east end was erected in memory of the twenty men of the parish who fell in the Great War of 1914-18. In 1887 a new organ was built and a carved oak reredos fixed, both the reredos and the chancel being enriched with subjects from the designs of Thomas Waters, a local artist. The church was completely renovated in 1902 and in 1907 a new carved oak reredos was presented by Dr. Mallins. In 1952 the cement rendering that had covered the flint work of the round part of the tower since Victorian times was removed to reveal very little damage to the flint work, which was then repointed to give a most pleasing effect to the fine craftmanship of the original builders eight hundred years ago.

In 1973 the bells were re-tuned and mention should be made of teams of hand-bell ringers, who for generations have given much pleasure, not only to the church congregation, but by ringing around the town during the Christmas Festivities.

A hundred new kneelers were made by the "Friends of the Church" in 1974 and the organ was restored in 1975 at a cost of £5,000. During 1978 the church heating system was completely overhauled. This involved the re-siting of the oil-fired boiler.

A most beautiful lectern, complete with steps and rails, were given to the church by the late Donald Moore in memory of his parents, the late Mr. & Mrs John Moore and Family and the late Mr. & Mrs. Fred Goss and family of Watton and were dedicated by the Bishop of Norwich on 20th July 1980.

October 31st 1983 was another memorial day in the history of St. Mary's Church, when the Bishop of Norwich the Rt. Rev. Maurice Wood again visited Watton to dedicate the extensive alterations to the church, recently completed at a cost of £25,000. Partitions of English Oak have been constructed to provide new and completely sound-proofed rooms at the rear of the wide aisles. Previously unused space in the north aisle has been converted into a rector's vestry, kitchen and toilet. The space at the rear of the south aisle which was formerly the rector's and choir's combined vestry, being divided from the rest of the church by a screen, has now been made into the choir's vestry and Sunday School Room.

The pews from the north aisle have been removed and the floor retiled, thus providing a multipurpose area for worship, exhibitions and meetings which has greatly increased the versatility of the church. The completion of this vast project marked the end of a six-year fund-raising period with most of the money being raised by the congregation. The work was executed by Gordon T. Hyde, a local builder.

# THE CONGREGATIONAL CHAPEL

*Congregational Church on Dereham Road.*

A Congregational Society was formed in Watton early in 1818, when according to a record in the Church Book to the effect "that it had plesed God in His mercy to inspire the heart of His servant, the Rev. Richard Fairbrother of Dereham, with a desire to relieve the spiritual destitution of the inhabitants of Watton and that upon inquiry he found five persons desirous of receiving, and aiding his benevolent design".

With the assistance of a neighbouring minister they started the movement by meeting for 'devine' worship in a cottage at Neaton where they continued until October 1818. From then until May 1819 Mr. C. Servier took over the ministry. Then with the addition of more members, a new Chapel was built at Neaton and was opened on the 3rd September 1819 when the Revs. Dewhirst of Bury St. Edmunds, J. Alexander and Hall, both of Norwich, and A. Creak of Yarmouth, took part in the services. This building served the Congregational Church under various ministers for the next thirty seven years. Then in 1855, during the Ministry of Rev. Alfred Griffin, a site nearer the town centre was obtained and it was decided to build a new Church. No time was lost in getting the project under way and surprisingly the foundation stone was laid by the Rev. John Alexander on April 3rd 1856. More surprisingly, this Gothic style church, which is still in use and stands on the Dereham Road, must have been built in record time as it is reported to have been opened by the above much respected Minister of the Gospel, with a special service on the 10th of August the same year. The walls are of black flint, with white brick dressings and the building extends to 48 feet in length and 27 feet in width. A school room was added at the rear of the church in 1862 and in 1871 a gallery was installed in the church, giving it accommodation for 300 persons.

Originally there was a turret at the south-west corner, but probably due to the high cost of maintenance it became dangerous and the upper half was removed about 25 years ago. When the new church came into use, the original one at Neaton was sold and converted into a private residence, later to become known as "Loch House", as it still is to-day. An interesting feature of the house is that the spiral staircase is believed to have been erected on the spot where the chapel pulpit stood and a part of the pulpit is thought to have been incorporated in the staircase. During the 1970's the Congregational Church became the United Reformed Church and was closed down from Easter Sunday 1976 (apart from one funeral service) but was reopened by The Assemblies of God in March 1977.

*Loch House was originally built for a Congregational Chapel and opened on 3rd. September 1819.*

# THE WESLEYAN CHAPEL

About the same period as the Congregational Church was opened at Neaton, a Wesleyan Chapel was built in Cley Lane, now known as Saham Road; during the hundred or so years of its life it had a somewhat fluctuating existence, suffering many a rise and fall of membership.

In 1870 its membership had diminished to such an extent that the Chapel was sold to a private owner. Interest however was aroused again after a few years and in 1881 the Chapel was repurchased. It carried on with varying success until 1933, when the Union of the Primitive Methodist and the Wesleyans took place, resulting in the Saham Road Chapel being closed.

# THE METHODIST CHAPEL

Methodism came to Watton in 1832 when Robert Key, described as a Primitive Methodist "Ranter", visited the town for the purpose of giving a sermon that hopefully would increase their following. From the various reports of the time, it appears that many in the assembled gathering on the Market Place were not too pleased to see him and he was therefore greeted with much abuse and harsh treatment. One report says the place was thrown into a state of unusual excitement and utter confusion. Another states that the speaker was twice thrown to the ground from his stand and was eventually taken to the George Hotel opposite in a semi-conscious state, where he was treated for his injuries and shock.

*Primitive Methodist Church and School Hall, Watton, 1928.*

However, it would appear that his oratory must have influenced some of the gathering, as shortly after a Mr. Took, who lived in a small house in "Worm's Yard", —but now known by the more dignified name of Beechwood Avenue—built an extension at the rear of his property which became the first Primitive Methodist Chapel in the town. This building appears to have been used as their Chapel for the next thirty years, when presumably the whole of it was again occupied as a private residence. Extensive alterations have recently been carried out on it and it has now been converted into Studio Khyber's new studio and shop.

In October 1862 the Primitive Methodist's trustees bought a plot of land in the High Street for £180 and the following year they commissioned the building of a new Chapel at a cost of £500. They had insufficient money to meet the full cost of the building, but fortunately a friend and benefactor, Mr. Mark Moore, of Saham Hills loaned them £250. A new schoolroom was added to the Chapel in 1874 and once again Mark Moore chipped in with another loan of £300 to complete this extension.

This Chapel served its purpose for the next 64 years, and now known as the Methodist Central Hall, is still in great demand for various social entertainments and the Women's Institute hold their weekly market there every Wednesday.

By 1913 the Chapel trustees were thinking about building another new Chapel and the adjoining land on which the old Maltings had stood for over 100 years was bought with this in view. Two years later it was thought this land was insufficient for their requirements, so a further ten foot strip was purchased for £25 and a wall was erected to enclose the disused maltings and all the land. Miss M. A. Moore was invited to lay the foundation stone in the east side wall and this she carried out on 1st July 1915, after which a tea was provided for all the congregation.

With the Great War now taking its toll of so many of the country's youth it was another eleven years before a start was made on the present Chapel.

Two foundation stones were eventually laid, one by the Primitive Methodist Church and the other by the Primitive Methodist Circuit, on 8th July 1926 and exactly one year later a large attendance saw the opening of the new Watton Primitive Methodist Church when the Rev. G. R. Brake, the resident minister, conducted the opening ceremony. Mr. M. G. Peeke-Vout, whose firm built the Church, handed the keys over to the Rev. Brake and the doors were subsequently unlocked by Mrs. G. Starling of Hilgay and Mrs. C. K. Fisher of Coney Weston, who declared the church opened for public worship. Upwards of 400 people then filled the church to overflowing to listen to the dedication sermon by the Rev. A. L. Humphries of Hartley College, Manchester, an ex-president of the Primitive Methodist Church. Teas were then served in the former church and in the schoolroom. In addition to the main building there is a minister's vestry and a large room for week-night meetings.

The seating accommodation in the church is 234 with an additional 50 in the gallery which is over the porch and lobbies at the front of the church. The financial statement, as presented by Mr. E. A. Harvey, indicated a total outlay of about £3,600, which includes alterations to the former church to adapt it for Sunday School work. £1,577. 18. 4d. had been raised previously and £176. 8. 4d. was taken on the opening day.

*This cottage in Worms Yard was the first Methodist Chapel in the town circa 1832.*

# THE POOR OF THE PARISH

The responsibility for looking after the poor was firmly laid on the parish by a Statute passed in 1597 and the parish was given the power to levy a poor rate through its overseers for the poor. Their accounts still survive in the town to-day in the Watton Parish Manuscripts. Further acts were passed at a later date that empowered parishes to purchase, or erect, buildings specifically for occupation by the poor and later still also for their employment. Thus a group of Watton people subscribed towards the erection of a house for the poor of the town when they met on 12th June 1719. They made an agreement with Ann Woodhouse, the Lady of the Manor, and her daughter, Ann Samwell, whereby for the payment of 1/- per year they could have a piece of land of the Manor of Watton Hall to build a dwelling house for the poor.

It was referred to as a "parcel of land and pasture of the common, or waste of the Manor of Watton, with an old house or cottage now built thereupon, near the end of Watton street running fifteen yards north to south and fifteen yards east to west (part of which is now enclosed) the said common pasture of Watton lying around the same cottage and land now enclosed Joseph Pannell dwelleth in—later in occupation of Thomas Fand".

This group also agreed on the same date to pay the Churchwardens of Watton towards building "a dwelling house upon the common pasture of Watton aforesaid for the use of the poor of the same parish or such other purposes as the parishioners shall from time to time think fitt". Thirty-one people subscribed £30 7s. 6d. with Mr. Scott being the biggest contributor with £4 and Robert Kiddell the lowest at 2/6.

The building accounts however are not very clear as one page lists a total sum of £32 9s. 9d. under the heading "a bill of disbursements about the Town House". Furthermore it appears that operations had already started in May 1719 as the first item was the payment of 4/6 for pulling down the house and clearing the ground. This referring to the cottage already built on the reclaimed land.

The town provided the timber that was to be used and Stebbing and boy were paid 10/- for felling it.

£2 14s. 0d. was paid for three thousand red bricks and £1 10s. 0d. for one thousand white bricks that were to be used. With a building 30 feet by 21 feet 2,500 bricks would be needed for the floor, so it would appear that the construction was of a timber frame, clay and wattle and daub on a brick plinth and brick floor. It can also be assumed that it had a thatched roof as the accounts show that the sum of £1 5s. 4d. was paid to a thatcher.

So by the end of 1719 Watton had, what appears to have been, its first "town house" where at least some of the poor of the parish could be given accommodation. The situation of the "Poor House", later to be called the "Workhouse", was near to what is now Graham Woodyatt's Fabrics Shop.

The parish manuscripts show the day to day issues that occupied the overseer for the poor as recorded in the overseer's books. Space prevents anything like a full detail of same being given, so only a few of the more interesting items will be mentioned.

The overseer had to keep a careful account of the income he received through the poor rate and of the money he spent. Francis Machin who was the overseer in 1769 collected £79 2s. 0d. for the six months starting 11th September, charging a rate of 2/4 in the pound.

It is possible to compile a list of the inhabitants of Watton wealthy enough to be rated, but not possible to tell where they lived, although the occupants of Neaton and the "Green" are listed separately.

Francis Machin himself was assessed at £2 and so had to pay 4/8 poor rate for six months. Mr. Francis Hicks paid the highest sum, nearly £13. Rev. Mr. Pigg paid £1 15s. 0d. for the vicarage (Willow House). The expenditure for the half year of 1769 was £89 1s. 6d. thus there was a deficiency of £9 19s. 6d., but the income from the town stocks appeared to have balanced the books. One wonders if the income had been as great as the expenditure, if this income from the stocks would have been shown?

A later entry reads, "playing the engine and mending the pipe £0 1s. 9d." Could this item apply to a town fire engine? Another odd entry is for "five yards of Russia Drab Thread, waxed, to mend the town Bede £0 6s. 6d." Would this refer to the repair of the Town Bible? It is therefore clear that expenditure on the poor and on general matters of town and church administration were not separated in the accounts.

In 1772 repairs and cleaning of the clock cost 8/1. More "flags" were cut in July and September, presumably peat, and the wheelbarrow was shod at a cost of 4/4.

The first intimation of the care of the sick by the community are to be found in the overseer's accounts for April 1773. At a town meeting held at the Crown on 12th April 1773, it was agreed that Mr. Robinson shall be paid by the overseers for the ensuing year, the sum of £7 7s. 0d. for looking after and attending the poor in the parish that are not charged in the rates. As it is Mr. Robinsons turn on the usual terms, it is agreed, if more sickness than usual should happen, that the parish will consider at the end of the year of some further satisfaction for him, and this appointment is understood to be for the ensuing year only and that midwifery is not included.

By 1796 one of my ancestors, William Jessup, was the overseer of the Workhouse and it is interesting to note from a copy of the original document what the weekly diet was at this period for the inmates. Below is a copy of the meeting held at the Crown on 4th October 1796:

*Crown Meeting Minutes 4 Oct 1796*

When the new Poor Law Amendment Act was passed in 1834, it aimed to make the condition under which the poor were to be helped discouraging, by insisting that help would only be given to those who went into institutions. The new institutions were to be set up on a wider basis than that of the parish.

Boards of Guardians were set up to administer the new Poor Law Unions. As no such Union had taken place in the Watton area, Watton's Town House and its almshouses, plus outdoor poor relief had to cope with the increasing poverty in the period after the Napoleonic War.

Mitford and Launditch Hundred were among the first to build one of these new institutions at Gressenhall, and it is the present Beech House Museum.

The "Hundred of Wayland" became the local unit for the operation of the New Poor Law in the Watton area and the first meeting of the Guardians of Wayland Union took place at the Angel Inn at Larling on 21st September 1835. Watton was represented on the Board by Mr. Smith Hastings and Mr. William Russell. By November of that year nine offers of land had been received and the Guardians instructed the committee to purchase a site of just over two acres near the Street in Rockland St. Andrew. The new Wayland Union Workhouse of brick foundations, solid clay walls and a slate roof was eventually completed a few years later with accommodation for 200 people. By the end of the century this building had clearly become far too small and in October 1911 the Board of Guardians invited tenders for a new building on a site near Attleborough. This building was completed by 18th May 1914 at a cost of £14,034 and is now the Wayland Hospital. Many extensions and improvements have obviously been carried out in the intervening years.

# THE ALMS HOUSES

In 1611 Edward Goffe of Threxton built 4 Alms Houses in the town. He died the following year and was buried at Saham Toney and the following clause concerning these Alms Houses was in his will, "I will that four of the poorest aged couples dwelling in Watton, shall have their dwelling in the alms-houses during the term of their natural life, and also an annuity of £5 per annum".

These houses were rebuilt in 1820 by Robert Harvey and housed many of the less fortunate townsfolk before they were demolished in 1958 and the site purchased by the Methodist Chapel for a car park.

Another of the town's benefactors was Edward Stevens who also built four Alms Houses in 1833 and in 1840 conveyed them to trustees for "The benefit of four poor married couples of the age of 60 years who have resided in the parish for not less than thirty years". These houses were completely modernised in 1975 at a cost of £15,000. They now have a modern sitting room, bedroom and a separate bathroom and are heated by electric night storage heaters. They are situated just west of Vincent Place.

*The "Stevens Alms Houses" built in 1833.*

# WILLOW HOUSE

Willow House is one of the oldest houses in the town, dating back to 1556. During it's long existence it has been used for a wide variety of occupations. In 1769 it was the vicarage and the incumbent was the Rev'd. Thomas Pigg and in all it was occupied by 13 vicars. It was also used as a private school, a boarding school, an antique shop and at the end of the first world war Mr. T. Baldry ran it as a restaurant with boarding accommodation and a billiard saloon. Following that, half of it was used as a laundry, and by 1926 it was a dentist's surgery and at this time a lock-up confectionery and tobacconist shop was erected on part of the front garden. This however was discontinued after five or six years.

A new Co-operative Stores was opened on another part of the front garden in 1928 and this building is now Rodney William's Gents Outfitters Shop.

The ancient Willow House was purchased by Modus Developments in 1973 when it was substantially modified, completely renovated and finally converted into one of the most attractive restaurants in the county.

*Willow House as it was in 1943.*

In 1977 it was sold to Mr. and Mrs. R. Callan and during the next year their business boomed to such an extent that they decided to invest in a new public house which would form an extension to "Ye Olde Willow House" restaurant. This was built of old materials, most of which came from a 400 year-old barn, with its fine oak beams being incorporated into the main structure. The walls and ceilings were also designed to give an impression of maturity. The exterior was likewise constructed so that the whole new building completely blends in with the existing property. The new Public House, which was named "The Tavern" was opened to the public on 23rd May 1978.

# HARVEY HOUSE

*Harvey House, built in 1720.*

Harvey House, one of the largest houses in the town was built in 1720 by Edward Harvey, who's father was Robert Harvey of Beachamwell. Their family were wool merchants who had connections in that trade at Downham Market, Hilborough, Rainthorpe and Norwich, to mention just a few places. John Harvey who founded the Norwich branch of the family was a worstead weaver, who was admitted a freeman of the City in 1695. Members of the Harvey family lived at Harvey House for many years and as mentioned under "Education", the town benefited from their generosity and from time to time the house was used as a school.

Later it became the residence and surgery of Dr's Panting, Sabonodiere, Plumbley and Dr. Shank's Group.

My first memories of Dr. Panting are seeing him being driven out of his drive in his pony and trap by Arthur Sturman who lived in the adjoining cottage and a year or two later he donned a chauffer's cap and drove the Dr. on his rounds in the latest in motor transport, a model "T" Ford car.

I have some painful recollections of his surgery, as I was taken there when I was 11 years old and had broken my arm and dislocated my wrist. Dr. Panting sat me in a high backed chair and instructed my father to stand behind the chair and put his arms around me so tight that I was unable to move. Having laid out a couple of splints and a few bandages he grabbed my arm at the elbow with one hand and my hand with his other and for the next minute or two he pulled and stretched my arm until finally he said, "That's it, did you hear the "click" when the bones went back into position". Being in considerable pain, I didn't hear anything, but wanting to be assured it was going to be alright, I said no, I didn't hear it. Very well then, I must do it again he replied and I really thought he intended putting me through this painful process once more, but my father saved me the agony by saying he had heard it and so the splints were placed in position, the arm bandaged and supported by a sling. No anaesthetic was given in those days for a broken arm, you just had to grin and bear it. During the last few years Harvey House has been the home of Mr. and Mrs. E. A Savory, but has recently been sold with Planning permission for a Nursing Home.

# PUBLIC SERVICES
## THE FIRE SERVICE

The first record of a Fire Engine at Watton that I have been able to find is of "A new Improved Carriage Fire Engine for 16 men". This was bought in 1845 by the efforts of the Threxton and Watton Fire Engine Subscription Fund as will be seen by the above copy of the original receipt. A Wayland Fire Brigade was formed in August 1890 and consisted of a Captain and 11 men and at this time the Fire Station was at the Wayland Hall and the garage where the engine was housed is now the Day Care Centre for the Elderly.

I can picture this old appliance now, which was worked by up to eight men pressing a long wooden handle up and down on either side of the machine. In fact, I helped to operate it on a few occasions when there was a fire during the day as when the firemen, who were on a part time retained basis, were at work anyone who happened to be about at the time lent a hand.

The main difficulty about the whole operation was getting the pump to the scene of the fire as it was hauled by a pair of heavy horses loaned for the occasion by one or another of the few firms who owned such animals at that time. Should a fire occur during working hours there was the problem of locating the nearest pair of horses and if it happened during off-work periods it could take even longer to get the pump under way. During the summer evenings this always presented a real problem as the horses would be grazing in a meadow and they soon learned that the sound of the fire bell meant extra work for them and they proved rather difficult to catch. Many a tale was told concerning this old fire engine. One of them being that a certain publican who supplied the fire brigade with much needed refreshments during their arduous task, was often at the scene of the fire with their refreshments before the firemen arrived with the pump.

Another story relates to a city gentleman who had come to live in the town to regain his health. Seeing a pair of horses approaching him hauling the pump up the High Street he doffed his hat, thinking it was a funeral cortege, whereupon a local called out to him, "Put yar hat on bor, that in't no funeral, thass our ole fire injin go'rn tu a fire". The gent replied, "In London our engines would be at the fire in two or three minutes". Not to be outwitted the countryman answered, "Yis bor, I know all about that, corse yar injin was pulled by an ole motor, but yu see, ours is pulled by tu ole hosses and them ole davels taake sum catch-un, as when tha' ole fire bell go they git rite acrost yun side a' tha' midder".

*The old Merryweather Steam Fire Engine was sold in 1937 and is here awaiting to be loaded onto a railway truck at Watton Station.*
*Back row left to right: — R. Wyer, R. Taylor, D. Moore, I Stokes, G. Goldsmith.*
*Front row: G. Peachment, W. Turner, B. Wyer and F. Hoy.*

This engine was replaced in 1925 by a Merryweather Single Cylinder Direct Action Steam Fire Engine with 1,300 feet of hose and was operated by a Captain, a Lieutenant and 7 men with the Parish Council now being responsible for its maintenance. The council applied to the Ministry of Health for a loan of £160 to pay for this engine, and in their reply they stated that having regard to the age of the engine they could not allow a longer period than three years for the repayment of the loan.

A report from the Norwich Union Fire Insurance Society stated that the engine was built about 1908 and their examination showed that "no repairs observed to be necessary".

Being steam operated, the first fireman to arrive at the station had to light the fire in the engine to obtain the necessary pressure to work it efficiently by the time it arrived at the scene of the fire and also to maintain the pressure during the time it was required to operate. The fire station for this engine was at the rear of Lloyds Bank. Like the previous one, it had to be transported to the fire, but the heavy horses had now given way to motor lorries and again private firms loaned their vehicles for this purpose until the council bought their own motor tender in 1936 for £47 10s. 0d. Following this acquisition, premises at the Green Man Inn were used for housing both engine, tender and all the equipment used by the brigade.

In 1937 the engine failed to meet the requirements of the Road Traffic Act and after a satisfactory demonstration a new Merryweather's "Hatfield Trailer Pump" size 1 was purchased by the Parish Council at a cost of £545 and the old Steam Engine was sold.

*Opening of the Fire Station, February 25th, 1961.*

With the outbreak of War the National Fire Service took over the control of fire fighting from the parish council and the station was then manned throughout the night and during the latter part of the war the pump and tender had to find yet another home, in premises belonging to the Bull Hotel. In 1948 the Norfolk Fire Service became responsible for fire fighting in the county and after years without a permanent fire station a purpose built one was opened on the Thetford Road on 25th February 1961.

The present engine is a Dodge E.R.F. Firefighter with Sub Officer Terry Cooke in charge and two leading firemen and seven firemen making up the crew. The Watton Fire Crew was awarded the Norfolk Efficiency Title for 1984, being the most efficient of the 36 on-call retained crews in the county.

December 20. 1845

The Treasurer to the Thwaxon Watton Fire Engine,
Subscription Fund.

To. W. I. Tilley
245. Blackfriar Road

| | | | |
|---|---|---|---|
| To a new Improved Carriage Fire Engine for 16 men with Patent Metallic Valves gunmetal Pistons and Cylinders, fixed in a well seasoned oak Cistern fitted with side Pockets for the Suction and Branch Pipes, a Box for the Hose &c, with a Driving Seat and Footboard. A Fore locking Carriage of Ash with Bar for front Horses and a Pole & a Droughandle, mounted on four best Steel Springs fay gorced Iron Axletrees, high wood spoke Wheels Painted Green, the Carriage Red & Varnished. | | | |
| 2 Copper Branch Pipes and 2 Gunmetal Jet Pipes. | | | |
| 2 Hose Wrenches. 1 Screwdriver. | | | |
| 1 Length of Copper Rivetted Leather Suction Pipe and gunmetal swivel screws lapped in do | | | |
| 1 Copper Strainer for do | £100 | .. | .. |
| To 1 Extra length of Copper Rivetted Leather Suction Pipe and gunmetal swivel screws lapped in do. | 2 | 18 | .. |
| To 2 40 feet and 1 20 feet lengths of Improved Leather Hose made with wrought Copper Rivets & moised tinned and 3 pairs of gunmetal swivel screws lapped in do. | 15 | 16 | 8 |
| To 6 large Copper Rivetted Leather Buckets @ 7. 0. 0 per doz | 3 | 10 | .. |
| To 3 doz. Canvas Buckets. @ £2. 14. 0 per doz. | 8 | 2 | .. |
| To Writing in Gold & shadow on both sides the Engine | 1 | 16 | .. |
| | £132 | 2 | 8 |
| Net Cash on delivery       Deduct | 2 | 17 | 6 |
| | " 129 | 5 | 2 |

*Accounts 20 Dec 1845*

# THE GAS WORKS

An important commodity in the form of gas was brought to the town in 1859. During the year large gas storage containers were erected on a site opposite the West End Stores and a house to accommodate the works manager was built adjoining it, in Cley Lane. Underground pipes were laid along the main roads of the town and the once familiar iron gas lamp standards were erected every hundred yards or so.

These had to be lit individually by the "gas man" walking, or cycling, around the town carrying a long pole with a hook on the end that enabled him to pull down a ring on the end of a chain, thus allowing a free flow of gas to set the small pilot jet in operation. This operation was carried out at varying times during the winter, according to the hours of daylight, but at 10p.m. every night his familiar figure could be seen again as he made his second journey of the evening around the deserted streets to extinguish the lights one by one. Several of the larger houses were also connected to the gas mains and thus for the first time in Watton's history, the more affluent residents were able to install a gas cooker. There were a number of by-products from the gas works, notably coke and tar, which found a ready market.

The former was coal half burnt and so deprived of its gases. It was then used as fuel by some of the business firms for heating boilers and the bakers also made use of it for heating their large ovens.

The tar was also in great demand, being used for waterproofing the clay lump cottages and for use as a binding medium and waterproofing the upper layer of shingle used in the construction of our earlier roads.

*The Gas Works and Manager's House was built in Cley Lane in 1859.*

37

# PUBLIC SERVICES

About the same time as the gas mains were laid along the main streets of the town in 1859 the first sewerage works were also constructed along Norwich Road, the High Street and Harvey Street. This was a large brick-built system that discharged the effluent into a sewer bed situated about 150 yards behind the gas works.

Although well over a hundred years old this brick system is still serving the town, but no longer in its original purpose, as it now acts as a surface water drain.

In the spring of 1951 contractors commenced work on the first stage of the new sewerage system for Watton and for the next few years there was much inconvenience to traffic as the various roads were ripped up and the main pipes laid along all the roads and finally to the new sewerage works that were constructed at Threxton.

With the completion of the first stage, no time was lost in getting the second stage on the way, this involved the connection from the individual properties to the mains and by 1957 this stage had reached the town centre, so it was nearing 1960 before all the properties were connected.

After having been illuminated by gas for 75 years, the old street lamp standards that had served the town were made redundant in 1934.

Much higher standards were then erected, the electricity poles that were to carry this form of street lighting to the town, and enabling those residents who so desired, to cook by electricity. The Eastern Electricity Co. supplied three lights per private house free of charge and any required above that had to be paid for by the householder.

In November 1935 Watton Parish Council received a letter from the Wayland Rural District Council informing them that a plan for mains water supply for the town and villages in the district had been drawn up and it was estimated that the daily consumption of water for the Wayland area would be 90,000 gallons for domestic purposes and another 50,000 gallons for business purposes, giving a daily total consumption of 140,000 gallons.

Where the rateable value did not exceed £5 the annual water charge per household was 10/- (50p) and above £6 rateable value it was to be 2/- in the pound of the rateable value. This was accepted by Watton Parish Council and the mains supply was laid in 1937-8.

The first telephone service for Watton was installed in the late 1920's. It was a manually operated system occupying Mrs. Utting's, the

Post Mistress's, living room and was operated by batteries housed in a shed in the yard behind the Post Office. The Post Office itself was No. 1. J. B. Abbey was No. 2, Barclays Bank No. 3 and H. G. Barnham & Son No. 4. An automatic exchange was built in Harvey Street in 1939-40 and from then on this system came into use in the town and district. The one exception being the late Lord Walsingham who did not wish to take advantage of the new system and had a direct line installed from his home to the Dereham exchange.

A new Police Station and Court House was built in 1954. Due to the centralisation of the local Courts in Norfolk, the Wayland Petty Sessions Division, which had sat at the new Court House since it was opened, was transferred to the Court Rooms at Swaffham in 1971.

Watton Parish Council held their meetings in the Court House until the building was opened on 22nd July 1973 as the Watton Branch of the Norfolk County Library.

A new Doctor's Surgery, built in the High Street in 1975 was opened on April 1st 1976. At the time of writing a new surgery is about to be built behind the new International Stores and this will all be on ground level, making it much more convenient for elderly patients.

# MEALS ON WHEELS

1968 saw the launching of a Meals on Wheels service when 14 elderly people in the town were provided with one meal a week at a cost of 1/6 a meal. Those responsible for starting this voluntary service were Miss K. Blomfield, Mr. B. Sharman and Mr. H. Hazel. In 1971 the service was extended to include the surrounding villages.

Originally the meals were prepared at the R.A.F. Station and later at the Wayland High School Canteen when 18 meals were provided twice a week, except during the school holidays, until 1979. Mrs. Marion Kittell become the organiser in 1972 and the cost of meals then was 11p but by 1978 it had risen to 32p.

In 1977 Mr. Garnet Mitchell suggested a scheme for developing the garages at the Wayland Hall to provide a kitchen for the Meals on Wheels service. Later the idea become more ambitious so that a lounge-dining room was built and a complete care centre instituted, which enabled people to come to the centre while others would continue to have their meals delivered by a team of volunteers. Dr. Shanks suggested that to complete the scheme the town should buy a minibus and this suggestion was taken up by Mr. Cyril Cadman.

Mr. Roy Rudling then started the ball rolling by opening the Mayor's Jubilee Fund which raised about £4,000. A community minibus was purchased and Mr. Cadman drove it to collect the first people to use the new centre on 29th, October 1979 and they were welcomed by Mrs. Ann Lusher, the Hostess.

Lady Walsingham officially opened the Community Care Centre on 8th January 1980, adding the final touch to months of hard work and planning by the Department of Health, Norfolk County Council, Watton Town Council and nearly every voluntary organisation in the area. Each week over 100 meals are now provided for the elderly.

After organising the Meals on Wheels service for 13 years Mrs. Marion Kittell retired in January 1985 and her successor is Mrs. Penny Harris, and Mrs. Rosemary Sharman is now the centre organiser. The service started with twelve voluntary helpers, later increasing to forty.

# THE RAILWAY

One of the most important events in the history of Watton was the opening of the Thetford to Watton railway line on 18th October 1869 by the Thetford and Watton Railway Company. Six years later the line was extended to Swaffham, when another privately owned Company, namely the Watton & Swaffham Railway Co., opened this stretch at a cost of £72,000. This section of line proved much more difficult to construct, as at Neaton, on the outskirts of the town, there was a very deep depression and to overcome this large quantities of soil had to be excavated to build up the banks that would eventually carry the line over this valley.

*Watton Station.*

The first train to run on this stretch of line was on 20th September 1875, but it was only used for carrying goods, as the safety authorities had yet to be satisfied that the new embankment was quite safe before passenger traffic was permitted. Within two months the line had been declared satisfactory and the first passenger service to Swaffham came into operation on 15th November 1875. The coming of the railway to the town brought much needed employment with the building of a house for the station master, goods, passenger and ticket offices, platforms, locomotive, carriage and goods sheds, a signal box, level crossing gates and the sinking of a well to supply water for the steam engines. Later, with two large cattle markets being established in the town, pens had to be erected near the station where the animals could be herded whilst awaiting loading onto the goods trains every

41

Wednesday. At the monthly sales, when many more cattle were entered in the markets, these pens were filled to capacity. Hundreds of crates of poultry, butter and eggs were also sent by train to London each week and hundreds of gallons of milk were also transported to the cities every evening.

Five passenger trains each way were operated on week-days and two on Sundays, and before the days of the motor car business people found the line a boon, enabling them to catch a fast train at Thetford, or Swaffham, to London and other large cities. Many generations of boys were also conveyed to both Thetford and Swaffham Grammar Schools and girls to the Girls' Grammar School at Thetford and the Convent School at Swaffham. Maybe it was one of the first of these pupils to travel on the train who named it "The Crab and Winkle", as it was always known to the locals. A familiar sight in the town for many years was Ted Grieves, the railway man, who with a horse and carriage and later a lorry, delivered the merchandise from the station to the town's many businesses.

A remarkable feature alongside one of the station platforms was a privet hedge that over a period of years had been clipped into the shape of a steam engine and the words "British Railways, WATTON" by Mr. F. J. Fagg, one of the railway porters. When the hedge was four feet high, in 1948, he started this work of art by gradually clipping out the word "WATTON" and over the next two years added "British Railways" and finally the steam engine. Everyone who saw it acclaimed it the finest piece of the topiarist art they had ever seen.

*Ernest Fagg and the privet hedge he created between 1948 and 1952 alongside a platform at Watton Station.*

*Last train from Watton, 1966.*

During the war years the Americans built extensive sidings at the station in order to cope with the vast amount of goods and equipment they brought in to keep their large air base working at full stretch.

With more and more people travelling by car after the war the "Crab and Winkle" line became one of the victims of Beeching's closure policy and the last passenger train on the line left Watton Station for Swaffham on the evening of 12th June 1964. About a year later the last goods train made its last journey and soon after the line was ripped up and the buildings demolished. Today the site of the railway and Tyrrell & Byford's grain and coal stores adjoining the station are now covered by factory units.

*The author, outside The Goods Enquiry Office at Watton Railway Station in 1921.*

*Swaffham Grammar School Boys waiting for their train. Back row, left to right: S. Harvey, W. Cross, S. Steward, E. Wright, F. Yaxley, Front row: J. Barrell, – Cason, E. Riches, "Tibby" Newton, R. Bird. Year 1931.*

# LOCH NEATON

When the Watton to Swaffham railway line was constructed in 1875 about a mile of its length had to be built up over low lying land at Neaton, then a hamlet adjoining the town. To form the embankment upon which the track was to be laid vast quantities of earth had to be excavated and this resulted in two holes of two to three acres being formed. The one nearer the town, on the west side of the line remained dry. The further one, on the east of the line adjoined the river Wissey and consequently soon filled with water. Following continuous frost during the severe winter of 1891 this sheet of water, known as the "Ballast Holes" was frozen to a great depth and a party of local skating enthusiasts decided to test its strength.

Having reached the railway bridge over the Dereham Road they climbed the embankment to take a short cut down the line. Included in the party was the local barber, familiarly known as "Teddy" Toombs.

Having enjoyed hours of invigorating sport they returned by the same route, discussing their enjoyment and regretting that there was not such an expanse of ice nearer the town. As they passed the dry hole Teddy remarked what an excellent skating arena it would make if only it could be flooded. His remark brought shrieks of laughter from his friends who said, "Where is the water coming from, and having got it, how could you keep it in"? You must be mad! These and other similar remarks and questions followed — no one ever dreaming that in a short period Teddy, with the help of his scoffers, would be creating Loch Neaton—but this is what happened.

After giving the idea more thought, he realised what a wonderful opportunity this spot offered for conversion into a pleasure resort. His imagination knew no bounds as he envisaged what could be achieved by plenty of hard work. Providing the hole could be made to retain water over a long period it would provide a skating arena in severe weather, a swimming pool and boating lake in summer, while fish could be introduced to provide sport for anglers.

The area surrounding the hole could be landscaped with trees and paths and there was sufficient room on the west side for a bowling green to be laid. The vital question was, where would the money come from to carry out such an ambitious project? Having talked over the idea with a few townsmen, George Durrant, a grocer and draper and Samuel Short, a baker, were convinced that it was an excellent suggestion and immediately offered financial assistance.

*Lower path and Boating Lake at Loch Neaton 1924.*

Having completed negotiations to obtain the land a start was made and after an enormous effort by voluntary labour, working up to their necks in clay to seal the bottom of the hole it was considered ready for water. Obviously many snags cropped up as the work proceeded, one was how to fill the area and keep the water at a sufficiently high level. Large pipes were laid to some low lying fields east of the railway line where surface water could be drained and channelled into the vast hole. This was not a success and then a locally made "Mill Pump" was tried, but again without success. A steam pump was next installed to pump water from a spring situated at the north end. This was reasonably successful, but the cost of working it was very high and it was therefore abandoned.

Mr. Short then went to look at a pump exhibited at the Royal Show at Cambridge and he was most impressed with it. Being wind operated the cost was negligible, so he purchased it and it gave many years satisfactory service.

The whole area became known as "Loch Neaton" and was run by a committee of townsmen. In March 1906 they received a most generous offer from Messrs Durrant and Short that in consideration of £200 being paid, the Loch would be conveyed to trustees on behalf of the town for all time, as a recreation ground. The offer was to close on Monday, 26th March 1906.

*Opening of the Band Stand, presented by
Miss Elsie Buscall to Loch Neaton 5.7.1906*

As secretary of the Loch committee, Mr. Thomas Adcock started to raise the money on Friday 23rd and by Saturday evening had collected over £250 in donations from most of the leading townsmen. Later that year Miss Buscall gave a most attractive Band Stand which was erected at the north-west corner of the Bowling Green and from then on Band Concerts provided a popular form of entertainment at this delightful setting for many years.

In the early days of its creation a strip of land beyond the band stand was set aside for playing quoits and some years later an additional piece of the adjoining farmland was acquired and four grass tennis courts were laid out and a rustic pavilion erected in one corner for the use of the players. A large pavilion was also erected in front of the bowling green and three changing apartments were constructed for swimmers. The one at the far end of the water was for men, a double one in the centre for ladies and girls and the one nearest the entrance for the use of boys. The depth of water was about two feet at the shallow end and rising to about eight feet at the deep end, where both high and long diving boards were installed.

*Ladies' Swimming Club, Loch Neaton.*

The entrance gate to the grounds was just before the railway bridge over Dereham Road and immediately in front of it steps were constructed in the embankment to the lower path which surrounded the water. By turning left at the entrance gate, a high level path curved its way round to the bowling green, while by turning right at the gate, the high level path presented a delightful panoramic view across the water to the water lily beds. A half dozen rowing boats were moored near the entrance during the summer months and could be hired by the half hour for a few pence per person. The banks between the two paths were planted with a variety of shrubs and in the spring parts of them were clothed with primroses and a number of rare wild flowers also found a niche here and there, including the beautiful mauve wood anemone. Looking back to pre-war days, when few people owned a car, Loch Neaton Pleasure Grounds provided many generations of townsfolk, and also the surrounding villagers, with endless hours of pleasure.

In addition to the various sporting facilties, mentioned elsewhere, special days, like Bank Holidays, always attracted large crowds when many additional entertainments were laid on. Two marathon races were held on Whit Mondays and created much interest and speculation weeks beforehand. The one for adults took the competitors over a five mile course round Carbrooke, Ovington and Saham and for those under 18 the course covered three miles. Both events attracted runners from all over the county and the starting and finishing point was at the entrance gate. On special occasions fairy lights were suspended from the trees around the water and were lit at dusk and displays of fireworks and dancing concluded the evening. Countless townsmen have given many hours of voluntary work at the "Loch" over the years for the benefit of all, but I feel a special mention should be made of Hubert Adcock's efforts during the last war that ensured Loch Neaton continued to provide much needed relaxation during those depressing years.

At the end of the war the water was drained from the whole lake and with the aid of American bulldozers which graded the bottom, a new swimming pool was formed at the far end by lining it with concrete walling. In 1962 this pool was converted into modernised baths 100 feet by 60 feet and included a diving well, a learners pool 1 ft. 6 in. to 3 ft. 6 in. deep, a children's splashing pool, spectator stands, changing rooms and a filtration plant at a cost of £11,000, a large sum for a small community to raise. A joint committee of the recreation ground and the Queen's Hall was formed and in 18 months £2,000 was raised for the cause by Saturday night dances alone. With the E.B.A. code of bowling fast gaining in popularity over the older E.B.F. game, the bowling green had to be extended to comply with the rules of the E.B.A. competitions. Once again this work was carried out by voluntary labour and with the extension completed, it enabled the bowls club to enter competitions under the E.B.A. code. But after several years it became obvious that other clubs were now constructing larger and more up-to-date greens and it was decided to create a new bowling green on the nearby sports field where there was room for a full size modern green adjacent to all the first class facilities already there. After much toil and sweat by an army of volunteers, the new green was opened in 1982 and the turf from the Loch Green was sold to Swaffham Golf Club.

By 1982 it became obvious that the bathing pool built in 1962 had reached the stage when considerable renovations had to be carried out, or a complete new pool constructed. A meeting was called to decide what action should be taken and as a result of this meeting a new committee was formed in 1983 under the chairmanship of Chris Edwards and they decided that a vast new building programme should be carried out. Despite the enormous expense this would involve, it was finally decided to create two new pools, one 12.5 metres by 25 m and the other 12.5 m by 7.5 m, complete with new changing rooms.

The committee were to provide all the materials with the man power services providing the labour. Various money raising programmes have been organised and to date £7,000 has been raised by voluntary efforts. A grant of £10,000 was made by the Town Council and a further £5,400 has been received from the Breckland District Council.

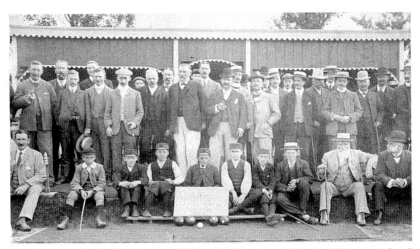

*Loch Neaton Bowls Club August 1905. Left of front row: Charles Robinson, right of front row in bowler hat is George Durrant, note the "Pill-Box "hats worn by the Bowls Wipers.*

*Loch Neaton Swimming Club, 1903. 2nd from left on back row: Percy Tennat, 4th from left: Ernest Jessup. Middle of front row: George Knott*

Demolition work started in April 1984 and the rebuilding commenced immediately after. The surrounds of the pools are now 75% complete, with the changing rooms up to damp course level. The pools have been designed with covering in mind and it is hoped also to have them heated in the not too distant future. Landscaping of the sides of the lake is to be carried out as soon as the pools are completed and in time it is hoped that a Band Stand and seating can be erected at the Dereham Road end. The whole project is a very large one and to date the cost is about £80,000 (including labour) and much more cash is urgently required to complete the programme.

*Loch Neaton.*

# EDUCATION

Education in Watton can be traced back to 1812 when there was a schoolmaster living in the town named Thomas Starke, but there does not appear to be any mention which school was under his headship. Certainly it was not the National School, as the first one was built in 1819 by William Robinson and consisted of one large room that was later divided into two by folding partitions. In 1842 it was in need of repairs and the opportunity was then taken to increase its capacity to accommodate 244 pupils by adding an Infants Room.

There was little space surrounding the school where the children could play, but in 1834 Mrs. C. Harvey generously gave a piece of nearby meadow land of some 2 to 3 acres to be used by "All children of Watton up to the age of 15 years" and three trustees were appointed to administer it. Forever after known as the "playpiece" it was used by countless Watton scholars for football, cricket, netball and as a training ground for the schools athletics into the 1950's. The generosity of Mrs. Harvey was extended to the school children over a number of years each Christmas, when she visited the school to present each child with a present, but it appears that there was no variation in the gifts, the boys always receiving a nightcap and the girls a red flannel petticoat.

*The National School, built in 1819.*

51

In addition to the National School—which incidentally is now Graham Woodyatts Fabrics Shop—there were a number of private schools in the mid 1800's. There were at least two periods when Willow House was used as a private school and during the school recess of 1847, Miss Blake, the mistress, had a number of alterations and improvements carried out so that she was in a position to announce on 3rd July that year that when the school reopened on 20th July she would be happy to receive her pupils and their increased accommodation would be complete.

By 1851 a school teacher named Mary Kett, whose husband was a grocer and draper, living in the High Street, organised another private school at Willow House and engaged Emily Harmer to be the music teacher. In 1854 Miss Ursular Wightwick resided here and ran it as a boarding school.

When the 1851 census was taken Elizabeth Targett and her sixteen year old daughter were both teachers, living in the Front Street, which was the middle part of the present High Street, on the South Side only. Also living in the Front Street in 1851 were Priscilla Alpe and her daughter Emma, again both school teachers. At this time Hannah Green was living in the School House and as no mention was made of her husband in the census, she was probably the Head Mistress and with Elizabeth Thompson, a schoolmistress living in Saham Road and a nineteen year old teacher named Charles Amos of Middle Row, may have completed the National School staff at this time.

Sarah Wright, who had a staff of two sisters, Eleanor and Elizabeth, ran another private school about this period, at Harvey House. A little later this school was taken over by Henry Goodwin, a Curate of Saham Toney, who with his wife Catherine educated five pupils who's ages ranged from 7 to 18. In 1877 Harvey House became a boarding school run by the Misses Knopwood. Dating back to the 17th century, "Six bright boys from Watton" were entitled to free education at Saham College, an important independent school through which these facilities were available by Trust.

Going back to the National School, we learn that Chas. Smith was the headmaster in 1854, but in 1871 Mr. Stace arrived from Sussex to take over the headship. By 1879 the schools most renowned and controversial headmaster of all time had been installed, while Mrs. Toombes, the wife of the instigator of Loch Neaton, became the assistant mistress. Yes, Charles Lintott was loved and respected by some pupils, disliked by others and feared by all. By the time I had progressed to the National School, Charles Lintott had retired, so I cannot give a personal account of him as an active schoolmaster. From what I have been told by many of his ex-pupils he was a strict disciplinarian, a supreme judge of their character, a great sportsman and merciless in his punishment for anyone who misbehaved. By this time much progress and change became apparent in the administration, and at a School Managers Meeting held in 1890 it was decided to revise the existing school fees which brought about some increases, thus: —

(a) Tradesmen and Farmers were to pay 3d. weekly for each child.

(b) Mechanics and journeymen to pay 3d. for the first child and 2d. for each subsequent child.

(c) Labourers, 2d. each for the first two children and any subsequent children to have free schooling. However, the following year the Managers adopted "Free Education", and carried out many improvements and additions. Separate teachers were appointed for each class, and an entrance door added for the younger children, new toilets were built and bay windows were built into the north wall.

An Infants School was built in the West End of Church Walk in 1876 with funds raised by public subscription. This accommodated about 60 pupils from the age of 5 to 7, when they were transferred to the National School. It was at this school that I started my education, at Easter 1917. The one large room was divided by a curtain drawn across a rail to form two classrooms with Mrs. Sykes, the Headmistress in charge of the 6-7 year olds.

There are one or two pupils still living in Norfolk who will remember our first morning at school when that kindly teacher, Mrs. Preston, gave us our first lesson, how to make animals from plasticine. Our two most memorable days at this school, were without doubt, the first and the last. The first was naturally a day of apprehension, the last because it so nearly ended in tragedy.

It was about a week after my 7th birthday in February 1919 and I remember it so vividly. We had only been back in school ten minutes after lunch when the late Ernest Codling thrust up his hand in desperation, saying, "Please teacher can I leave the room". "No', replied Mrs. Sykes, "you should have used the toilet before you come in". With his face becoming whiter every second, he repeated his urgent request, to which the head mistress replied, "Well, be quick boy, if you must go". During the few minutes he was away a few of us heard a faint rumbling noise close to where I was sitting, at the east end of the room. Upon his return he immediately called out, "Please teacher the school is falling down". This remark annoyed the teacher and she threatened him with the cane, whereupon another boy and myself informed her that we had just heard a rumbling noise. Even then she was not convinced of any danger, but no doubt observing the serious look on our faces, left the room to investigate. Dashing back into the room she ordered everyone out immediately. Leaving us in the care of Mrs. Preston, she set off to inform the Rev. C. Nash, who was chairman of the school managers, but before she was fifty yards away the whole of the east end and a large part of the north wall had collapsed.

Had Ernest Codling not have had a "call of nature", I am certain that several girls and boys would have been killed that afternoon. All the scholars were given temporary accommodation in the Parish Room until Easter, when we were transferred to the "Big School" as the National School was known to us youngsters.

A year in Standard I with Mrs. Toombs as our teacher was followed by a further year with Miss Gaze in Standard II, before being transferred once again to what was officially known as "The Temporary Provided School". This was a series of ex-World War I wooden army huts where everyone was roasted in summer and frozen in winter - hardly the best environment to study for examinations. This is where my age group finished our schooling, at Easter 1926. Those pupils who resumed school at Watton after Easter were fortunate to go into a fine new brick built school with what was at the time, the very best in school facilities.

The site for this school was bought in 1920, but owing to the very high cost of building just after the war, the new building was shelved until 1925-6. This new school then had accommodation for 152 pupils with a teaching staff of five and was formally opened on 13th April 1926 by Mr. A. G. Copeman, the Chairman of Norfolk Education Committee and was to be known as Watton Senior Mixed Council School. Since then it has been enlarged twice and is now the Junior School with 280 pupils and a teaching staff of twelve.

One interesting memory that I have of my days in the "Temporary Provided School" was the six-monthly visits of the school dentist who used to arrive in a romany type van pulled by a horse. During the summer months it became so hot in the van that the dentist left the door wide open, thus enabling the children to watch the sufferings of the patient in the "dreaded chair" from the bottom of the caravan steps. He appeared to sterilise his instruments of torture over a primus, or similar type stove, before commencing operations. Whilst this was going on the horse was ever on the look out for a meal and in the absence of grass, the school hedge supplied the main course, with rose bushes in the adjoining garden providing "the sweet" which was often followed by bread and cheese supplied by the children from their lunch tin and on at least one occasion a girl's woolly hat disappeared in mysterious circumstances.

On Tuesday, November 18th, 1958 the new Secondary Modern School, which had been in use since Easter, was officially opened by Mr. F. R. Salter, Warden of Madingley Hall, Cambridge. Addressing the 490 pupils he said, 'A School of this sort is a delight, a challenge and a temptation and it was a shining and burning light through East Anglia".

Since then the school has been considerably extended and a new era in secondary education at Watton started on Monday, September 6th, 1976 when some 190 children from the town and nearby villages became the first students in the all-ability system.

As from 1st September 1976 Watton Secondary School became Wayland High School. Watton was one of only six Norfolk Schools selected as the first in the county to "go comprehensive". The new term started with 760 pupils on the roll. Today there are 840 pupils with a teaching staff of 47.

On July 4th 1979 the new Westfield First School was officially opened by Mr. David Coatesworth, the County Education Officer. All the 240 pupils of the school were given a tagged balloon which they released into the air upon a signal given by Mr. John Edwards, area education officer.

The numbers of pupils and staff are variable from year to year at all the schools and the present figures for Westfield First School are 180 pupils and a teaching staff of 7. During the 1920's Miss Denton ran a Private School in part of the premises belonging to Lloyd's Bank and upon her retirement Miss Nora Wace continued to run it in the 1930's.

*Boys and girls outside the National School, circa 1889. Note both the boys and girls are wearing "hob-nail" boots.*

# CROWN HOTEL

The "Crown Hotel" was built around 1760 and is characteristic of this period. In its heyday, 1850 to 1892, it became one of the best known hotels in the country, not only for the excellent quality of its beer and spirits, but also because the proprietor, George Jacobs, was not only a publican, but also a reputable horse breeder and dealer.

Providing stabling accommodation at the Crown for about 200 horses and another 150 at the west end of the town, made him one of the largest horse breeders and dealers in Britain. He was reputed to have started his dealing business by buying and selling a donkey. He had his own blacksmiths shop adjoining the stables at the Crown and employed some twenty hostlers, also his own horse doctor, or veterinary surgeon, as he would be known today.

Customers came from all over England as well as abroad and included the King's of Austria and Italy.

During the latter part of his life, when he was confined to bed, he decided to "run down" the number of horses and it is said that he disposed of most of them to visiting customers by having a hostler run a horse up and down the High Street a few times which enabled him to assess its value from the sound of its trotting which he could hear plainly through the open bedroom window. Having reduced his numbers to sixty-six in this way, the finest of his famous stud of Carriage Horses and Norfolk Hackneys were sold by auction at the Crown Hotel on Wednesday 6th April 1892 as will be seen from a few extracts of the sale catalogue. It will be noted that 34 of them were bred by himself from selected mares and a few of the others were bred by another reputable horse breeder, William Welsher, who farmed at Carbrooke, Griston and Watton.

The Great Eastern Railway advertised a train service in the sale catalogue from Liverpool Street, Doncaster, Lincoln, Norwich, Cambridge and Newmarket.

After the First World War the Crown entered a new phase in its long history when R. G. Holmes converted part of the stables into the first garage in the town for selling and repairing motor cars. This was opened in August 1919 and for the next decade it was the largest garage in the district. A new wing was added to the hotel about 1930, making it by far the largest in the town. Following the death of Richard Holmes Junior, the hotel was sold and on 1st July 1949 a disastrous fire gutted much of the building and despite the efforts of three fire brigades every window facing the street was shattered and the roof was open to the sky. Fortunately, no one was injured but many escaped in the nick of time and lost all their personal belongings. A few years later the car show room, facing the street, was converted into a cafe, but after a few more years this also was destroyed by fire. It then stood derelict for many years, creating an eyesore in the town centre until it was demolished completely. This site now forms part of the imposing approach to the new International Stores and King's Chemist Shop.

*George Jacobs, the well known Horse Breeder and Landlord of the Crown Hotel with his wife and daughter circa 1885.*

*Taxicab picking up a fare 1880*

UNRESERVED SALE
OF
GEORGE JACOBS' STUD OF

# CARRIAGE HORSES

AND

## Norfolk Hackneys,

AT

WATTON, NORFOLK,

By direction of Mr. GEORGE JACOBS.

WEDNESDAY, April 6th, 1892.

G. M. SEXTON,
Auctioneer,
Stone Lodge, Ipswich.

*Carriage Horses*

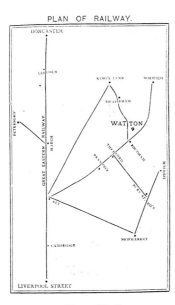

DONCASTER

LINCOLN

KING'S LYNN    NORWICH

SWAFFHAM

WATTON

THETFORD    ROUDHAM

BRANDON    BURY ST ED'S

IPSWICH

GREAT EASTERN RAILWAY

PETERBORO'    MARCH

ELY

CAMBRIDGE    NEWMARKET

LIVERPOOL STREET

*Plan of Railway*

# 66 HORSES,

CONSISTING OF

**27** Carriage & Brougham Horses, Harness Horses and Cobs,

**9** Hackney Stallions,

**19** Hackney Brood Mares,

**11** Three and Two-year-old Hackney Fillies,

To BE SOLD BY AUCTION, AT THE

## CROWN HOTEL, WATTON,

*Wednesday, 6th April, 1892.*

PUBLIC LUNCHEON at 12.30, Sale immediately after.

Auctioneers:

SEXTON and GRIMWADE,
Ipswich and Colchester.

SALTER, SIMPSON & SONS,
Attleboro'
*(Jointly concerned).*

*Catalogue of 66 Horses*

| | | | |
|---|---|---|---|
| *Leave* Liverpool Street | .. | 5.55 a.m. | 9.10 a.m. |
| ,, St. Pancras | .. | — | 9.15 ,, |
| ,, Ely | .. | 8.57 ,, | 11.5 ,, |
| ,, Thetford | .. | 9.41 ,, | 11.56 ,, |
| *Arrive* Watton | .. | 10.13 ,, | 12.42 ,, |

| | | | |
|---|---|---|---|
| *Leave* Ipswich | .. | 8.2 a.m. | — |
| ,, Bury | .. | 8.45 ,, | — |
| ,, Thetford | .. | 9.30 ,, | — |
| *Arrive* Watton | .. | 10.13 ,, | — |

| | | | |
|---|---|---|---|
| *Leave* Peterboro' | .. | 7.10 a.m. | 9.30 a.m. |
| ,, March | .. | 7.57 ,, | 10.21 ,, |
| ,, Ely | .. | 8.57 ,, | 11.13 ,, |
| ,, Thetford | .. | 9.41 ,, | 11.56 ,, |
| *Arrive* Watton | .. | 10.13 ,, | 12.42 ,, |

RETURN TRAIN.

| | | |
|---|---|---|
| *Leaves* Watton | .. | 4.51 p.m. |
| *Arrives* Liverpool Street | .. | 8.30 ,, |

*Train Service*

## Hackney Stallions.

Lot 30.

**Watton Delight** (2760)—Chestnut. 15.1 h.h. Foaled 1888.

Breeder, George Jacobs, Watton.

*Sire*—1 MID NORFOLK SWELL (2594)
*g.-Sire*—CONFIDENCE, D'Oyly's (158)
*g.-g.-Sire*—PRICKWILLOW (614)
*g.-g.-g.-Sire*—FIREAWAY PRICKWILLOW (229)
*g.-g.-g.-g.-Sire*—PRICKWILLOW (607)
*g.-g.-g.-g.-g.-Sire*—NORFOLK PHENOMENON (522)
*g.-g.-g.-g.-g.-g.-Sire*—NORFOLK COB (475)
*g.-g.-g.-g.-g.-g.-g.-Sire*—FIREAWAY (208)
*g.-g.-g.-g.-g.-g.-g.-g.-Sire*—FIREAWAY (203)
*g.-g.-g.-g.-g.-g.-g.-g.-g.-Sire*—FIREAWAY (201)
*g.-g.-g.-g.-g.-g.-g.-g.-g.-g.-Sire*—DRIVER (187)
*g.-g.-g.-g.-g.-g.-g.-g.-g.-g.-g.-Sire*—SHALES THE ORIGINAL (699), foaled 1755

1 MID NORFOLK SWELL won Prizes in 1888 FIRST as Three-year-old and FIRST as Coach House Mid-Norfolk and East Dereham Show.

*Dam* by Beaconsfield (1709) by Lord of the Manor, Smith's (426) by Goldfinder, Rice's, by Black Rattler, Harrison's (82) by Performer, Ramsdale's (547)

Lot 31.

**Watton Hero** (2761)—Bay. 15.2 h.h. Foaled 1888.

Breeder, George Jacobs, Watton.

*Sire*—MID NORFOLK SWELL (2594), see Lot 30
*Dam* by Lord Beaconsfield II. (2153) Lot 34, by Beaconsfield (1709)

*Hackney Stallions*

59

# WAYLAND HALL

The Town Hall, or as old Wattonians have always known it, Wayland Hall, being named after the hundred in which Watton is situated, stands on the Market Place and was built in 1853. At the time of its erection it was described as a handsome brick and stone building in the late Perpendicular style. The ground floor consisted of a lofty reading room, waiting room and other offices from which there is an ascent by a stone staircase to the room appointed for the magistrates. Also on the upper floor is a large room constructed for the purpose of a corn hall, assembly and concert room.

The roof is of open timber work with hammer beams and spandrels cut into open tracery and completed with large panes of glass. The large windows are framed so as to be in perfect keeping with the general character.

The building surely fulfilled a great public need in the town at this time as previous to its erection farmers and merchants had no suitable place where they could meet to barter their produce and those convening meetings or arranging social events were always in a quandary as to where to hold them.

*Watton Ancient Order of Foresters at Dinner in Wayland Hall, Watton on Whit Friday 1907. Fourth from left in front row G. Bowden, seventh: E. Jessup.*

The Wayland Petty Sessions, which were held fortnightly on a Wednesday, had a court room at the Crown Hotel one year and at the George Hotel the next and this was considered most unsatisfactory, but with the opening of the Town Hall they were transferred to a Magistrates Room in the new building.

Many a man who was summoned to appear before the magistrates for such minor offences as riding a cycle without lights found himself the target of jest by his friends, who informed him that he would be very fortunate if he got away with a fine of less than a 1/- a step. As there were over twenty steps to the magistrates room it was quite a relief when the case was over and a modest fine of 5/- was all that was imposed.

For many years Wayland Hall was found adequate for what it was intended, but its use as a corn hall steadily declined and a few years ago the glass roof was replaced by tiles.

The large room has been the venue of a great variety of activities in the past including boxing tournaments, dances, Christmas Parties, dinners, auctions, theatrical plays, concerts and badminton. Older residents will also remember many a lively political meeting held there. In 1930 this room was converted into a cinema where the first talking films were shown in the town, until the new Regal Cinema was opened in 1938.

For the next few years it was again used for social activities before being sold to the Norfolk County Council and converted into one of the finest public libraries in the county and opened in November 1950. Towards the end of the 1970's it was purchased by Watton Town Council and it now houses the Council Chamber, Town Clerk's Office, Day Care Centre, Kitchens for the "Meals on Wheels Service", Social Services, Register Office, Wedding Room, Job Centre Officer, a Breckland District Council Officer and a Citizens Advice Officer, while the large room once again provides a venue for many social activities as in the past.

An interesting item housed in the Town Clerk's Office is the Silver trowel used in the Stone Laying Ceremony of the hall. On one side is an engraving of Wayland Hall as it was when built and on the reserve side the engraving reads, "Presented to the Lady Walsingham on her laying the foundation stone of the Wayland Hall, Watton, April 26th 1853".

In July 1982 an oil painting of the U.S. 8th Army Air Force emblem was presented to the Town Mayor, Mrs. Janis Crabtree, by Ken Godfrey on behalf of the Americans who were stationed in Watton nearly 40 years ago. This painting, together with a plaque, now has a place of Honour in the Council Chamber.

# "THE WATTON ALMANACK AND ADVERTISING MEDIUM OF 1891".

A copy of the "Watton Almanack and Advertising Medium of 1891" was discovered by one of the town's businessmen when carrying out alterations to his shop a few years ago and it makes most interesting reading. As there are a number of tradesmen mentioned therein whose family business is still being carried on by their founders third, fourth, or even fifth generation we thought that it would be of great interest to most readers and bring back many memories to the older Wattonians. New comers to the town will also find much of interest in these adverts, not least the prices of ninety-four years ago, but also in the wording of the various advertisements. This reflects how very competitive they were, offering a wide variety of inducements to patronise their shops with free delivery to all surrounding villages being offered by some tradesmen. By far the largest shops in the town at this time were Messrs Durrants's, Kendall's and Dunnett's and the former is still in business with the third generation of the family running it.

*W. Kendall*        *The Watton Almanak*

It will be noted that W. Kendall's West Norfolk Supply Stores supplied grocery, drapery, hosiery, boots. shoes, millinery, men's, boys and children's wear. Also, with their "New Modern-built Hearse with Glass Sides", they offered Funerals completely furnished. In fact, one could say they catered for the inhabitants from the cradle to the grave. Today this shop is now the large hardware, homecare and china store of Julnes & Sons.

George C. Durrant was a Tea Dealer, provision Merchant, Dressmaking, Millinery and also had a mourning Department with a "New Hearse" at the "GREAT SHOP". At this period Durrant's employed a staff of over fifty, and twenty of them were dressmakers who lived on the premises. As a very young boy, I can still picture George Durrant standing at the shop door in a bowler hat, long coat and slippers. He opened the door in his friendly manner for each customer and as they were about to leave he always asked if they had been suited, and if not, would endeavour to obtain whatever they required as quickly as possible. He was one of the two gentlemen who financed the development of Loch Neaton and his grandson is still carrying on the family business and has also given many hours of his time for the Loch Swimming Pool, painting the whole of it on his own a few seasons ago. The property, built between 1761 and 1787, is one of the oldest in the High Street. All of it, as well as some others, were owned by the wealthy and influential Youngs family and a monument to them can be seen in St. Mary's Church dated 1770-1805. Besides an extensive grocery and drapery business, they were also brewers and later there was a "Tallow Chandlers" at the rear of the shop until the whole estate was sold in several lots on November 11th 1839.

*Durrants – Come to this shop*

*Durrants – To the Inhabitants of Watton*

The Durrant and Kendall families were friends, but George and William were keen business rivals and they made regular checks on each others prices. Each had built up a great number of regular customers and by means of extended credit and personal attention, kept them. Perhaps George's were more church than chapel and William's the opposite. In due course they provided a funeral for their customers and keenly competed for the business of those who were not. One day George was arranging the funeral of somebody who William considered to be his by right. After the service at the Methodist Chapel, William, complete with walking stick, was standing on the kerb next to the horse. The coffin was being loaded, but before the hearse door could be shut, the horse bolted, causing the coffin to be dropped in the road. The driver could not pull the horse up and it reached the railway crossing gates in Church Road, where fortunately, the gates were shut for the arrival of the train and this enabled the driver to gain control. The local populace were treated to the sight of an empty hearse galloping up the High Street only to return a few minutes later. The coffin was duly collected and the funeral proceeded at its befitting pace. William Kendall was heard to remark, "What a way to conduct a funeral".

D. Dunnett's shop was situated along the north side of High Street, across the Market Square to the south side of Middle Street and occupied the premises where Charrington's Fuels, Hilton's Shoe Shop, Dewhurst's Butchers, Preston's Book Shop and the Middle Street Dressmakers now trade. Like Durrant's and Kendall's, Dunnett's also dealt in grocery, provisions, hosiery, boots, shoes, drapery, millinery and in 1891 the price of their "WATTON WONDER" Tea was only is 2d. per lb. The Special Report of a Meeting held at H. Adcock's renowned "West End Stores" makes interesting reading, as will be seen on page 71. This shop is still operating on the same site and is still a grocers.

*Dunnetts – General & Fancy Drapery*

*Dunnetts - Outfitting*

Adcock & Sons, Builders, contractors and undertakers etc., were followed by Harvey's then by W. Peeke-Vout & Son, who built the Methodist Chapel. All had their works and offices where the residential site of Vincent Place now is.

A.W. Julnes - "The Poor man's Friend" - was a coal and coke merchant, also a dealer in rags, skins, horse hair, metal and iron. Two items of special interest in his advert are that he was prepared to take in any old iron, lead and other metal in exchange for coal. As times were very hard then, with little money to spend, many people would have been glad of this offer, as no doubt they could often manage to collect a few of these items to exchange for coal. More interesting still was the notice to hawkers - "Wanted 100,000 dozen Rabbit Skins", or in other words one million, two hundred thousand. This clearly shows how many rabbits there were in the sandy Breckland area right on our doorstep and also how many people in those days relied heavily on the rabbit to provide a cheap, nutritious and delicious meal. Julnes's business at this time was situated on the corner of Norwich Road and Church Road, where Dye's now display many of their cars. When I first remember them they were also corn merchants, in fact, by then it was probably their largest turnover. They also had a coal yard at the station and a small shop in High Street where they sold seeds and pet foods, as they still do today, but this shop has been vastly extended and modernised in recent years. It is also one of the oldest properties in the High Street, dating back to 1769.

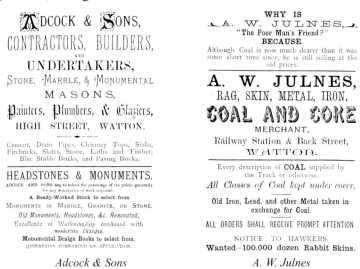

*Adcock & Sons*

*A. W. Julnes*

E. F. Toombs, Hairdresser and Perfumer was the gentleman who had the wonderful idea of creating Loch Neaton Pleasure Grounds that have provided so much pleasure to many generations of Watton's inhabitants. His shop was where Weston's Cake shop was until last year and is now "Alf's Cabs and Tea Caddy".

Sam Short, the baker who was the other gentleman who financed the lay-out of the Loch Neaton Pleasure Grounds had this unique advert in the Almanack: - "His biscuits were good for the temper, his bread good for the stomach and baking powder that was good for the complexion". He should have done a flourishing trade in these wonderful aids. Later, John Moore and his son Donald carried on the bakers business and their shop and bakery is now displaying the latest in kitchen and bathroom equipment at the corner of Dereham Road.

In addition to selling stationery, toys and fancy goods, John Edwards was also a photographer and Bird Preserver and many an old picture in the town today was framed by him. His great grandson, Chris, is still carrying on in the same shop which in the last few years has been extensively extended, as will be seen by comparing the old and recent photographs of the shop.

Lacey Vincent's Chemist, Druggist and Wine and Spirit Merchant's shop adjoined the Clock Tower, and will be remembered by many older Wattonians. Upon his retirement the business was bought by Jas. Horsburgh and he and his son Deric, carried on there for many years and later it became Watton Pharmacy until King's Chemist was opened on the opposite side of the street on 11th September 1984. It will be noted that in 1891 Vincent's were offering Ale and Stout in 18, 9 and 4½ Gallon Casks at 1/- (5p.) a gallon. They also made their own special cures like Balsom of Honey for all chest complaints and "No sheperd should have been without Vincent's 'Powder's for Ewes' during the lambing season". Lacey's brother Percy became Lord Mayor of London in 1936.

Stace & Harvey were Printers, Bookbinders and Copper Plate Engravers, later becoming Harvey & Sons, Printers and Stationers and are another long established Watton firm that is still in the same business and now being managed by the third and fourth generations of their family.

*A Postcard sold by Harveys 1903*

*Stace & Harvey*

*Lacey Vincent – Chemist & Druggist*

*Lacey Vincent – Chemist*

Another very old Watton firm was Henry Siggins who became established in 1840 and had their Plumbing, Glazing and Decorating business at the junction of Harvey Street and Dereham Road, where Martin Anscombe's "POP IN" was until recently. Their business finished soon after the last war as there were no descendants in the family to carry on.

George Butcher's General and Furnishing Ironmongers business used to be where Roy Rudling's D.I.Y. Store now stands.

James Garner's Agricultural Engineers and Blacksmiths was another long established firm whose works were situated where Noel Dye now displays his Tractors and William Crane was apprenticed there at the age of 13 and retired at 70, having completed 57 years with the same firm, a fine record.

*Waters & Sons, Builders were established in 7853.*

*Waters & Sons Plumbers & Decorators*

*Geo. Butcher*

Waters and Sons, Plumbers, Decorators and General Builders etc., was established in 1853 with works in the High Street and Norwich Road, later moving to larger premises on the Thetford Road. Following the death of Dan Waters in the 1950's, his son Deric took over the business for a short period before deciding to take a post in Hong Kong, where he became the Principal of the Morrison Hill Technical Institute, retiring in 1980 as Assistant Director of Education for Hong Kong. Since 1974 the business premises have been occupied by Aspect Special Products Department, where a dozen men are employed in the production of Special Roofing Tiles.

As shown in the above advertisement, the Watton Brewery was established in 1809, but it was not until 1831 that a small part of the building still standing in the High street was built by Edward Stevens, probably on the site of the earlier and smaller works.

His son Robert extended it in 1838 and managed it until his death in 1866. It was later purchased by Thomas Crawshay Frost and under his guidance the business expanded considerably so that in 1877 he built a large extension that doubled the brewery's output.

This work involved the erection of a much larger chimney that completely dominated the look along the sky line in the High Street until it became unsafe and was demolished in February 1975. Older residents claim that Watton had three wonderful wells that supplied a constant supply of excellent water to many of the inhabitants, either directly, or indirectly, until the mains supply arrived. One was under the Town Pump by the clock tower, another by the National School Pump and the third was in the brewery yard and until a few years ago several residents could remember this well and the horse that operated the machinery that pumped the water into the brewery, where it was used in the brewing of the beer.

Crawshay Frost sold the business about 1890 to William Cann and Co., of Wymondham and later it was acquired by Morgans Brewery of Norwich, who continued to brew beer in the town until about 1912. When Mr Frost was living at the Brewery House - now the "Chocolate Box" - it was his custom on Valentine's Day to collect a hundred or so new pennies from the Bank and after heating them on a dustpan over an open fire until nearly red hot, he threw them out of an upstairs window into the street for the children to scramble for and many a small finger got burnt in the fun. Today the brewery is occupied by the well known firm of Rapide Printing Works.

*West End Stores Meeting*

# THE WAYLAND SHOW

Watton Show must surely be one of the first agricultural shows to be held in Norfolk, having originally started in the 1790's as a show for cottage garden and home produce, but by the turn of the century there were a few classes for cattle and farm crops. From the old minute books that I have seen the most interesting class then was for "The best pair of Working Oxen". An entry in the show minute book for the 6th November 1851 reads, "That the Rt. Hon. the Lord Walsingham be requested to continue the Office of President of the Society". It is reasonably certain that successive Lord Walsingham's have been the Show's President from its inception right through to the present time.

In a report of a show committee meeting held in 1856 it was decided to withdraw the class that year for the "Best two working Devon Bullocks". Presumably by that time horses had almost completely taken over the ploughing from the oxen. By this time there were classes for horses, cattle, sheep, pigs, poultry, rabbits and the usual farm crops of mangel-wurzels, swedes and turnips.

My own memory of Watton Show, as it was usually referred to in those days, goes back to 1919, but for a number of years it was called the Wayland Exhibition and for many years now, the Wayland Agricultural Show.

Between the two world wars it was always held on the two meadows now occupied by the Library, Police Station, George Trollope, East, West, North and South roads. The entrance to it was through Mr Goddard's farm yard, where the veterinary surgery is now. At this time it was always held one Wednesday, usually between 10th and 22nd September, the actual date being governed by the anticipated date that the harvest would be completed by and fixed accordingly. Although due to our unpredictable weather this did not always work out satisfactorily and when the show was held before the completion of harvest it seriously affected the attendance.

In the 1920's Watton Show Day was the only day's holiday many villagers and farm workers had each year, so it is only natural that they looked forward to it weeks ahead and great was their disappointment if the harvest was not completed before the day, as many farmers insisted that the harvest must come first and both men and master then missed the show. This probably happened in 1879 when the takings on the gate were only £3 l0s. 4d.

Either directly, or indirectly, all the agricultural community looked for a good harvest each year as times were very hard in those days and if the corn was not harvested in good condition everyone felt the pinch.

For many years it was customary for the show officials, their guests, judges and members etc., to partake of lunch in a large marquee when the main course was traditionally "Pigeon Pie". This item was withdrawn from the menu in the late 20's.

*A Show Day scene in the High Street in the late 1800's.*

Boys of my generation looked forward to "show day" for weeks ahead and many of them registered their names with Sidney George, the Show Secretary, long before the day, to be considered for such tasks as programme selling, or that of escorting the judges of the various classes, carrying the coloured rosettes which they handed to the judge for tying on the selected winners. This job carried a higher status and the genial secretary allocated this important task to the older boys who had given satisfaction as programme sellers in previous years.

Since the last war most show days have been held on a Saturday, or Sunday, and the records will show that attendance figures have been broken on a number of occasions since the show was held on Wednesdays. What the records will not reveal, however, is that in pre-war days the number of visitors attracted to the town on show days far exceeded the numbers that visit the town now. Just about everyone from a 12 mile radius came to Watton on show day, most of them on cycle and about one house in four in the town displayed a notice, "Cycles stored here 3d.". The farmers and their families came in their horse and traps and even as long ago as 1878 the Thetford and Watton Railway Co. advertised return tickets at single fares from Bury St. Edmunds, Thetford, Swaffham and all stations along the line.

*Winner of the Society's Prize for the Best Steer, not exceeding 15 months old, at the Wayland Agricultural Society's Show, Watton, 1903. Mr. J. Jessup, Redhill Nursery Farm, Watton.*

Many of the visitors, however, never reached the show ground, preferring to spend the day in the public houses or along the High Street and Market Place where there were a great variety of attractions including so called "Cheap Jacks", "Quack Doctors" and "Smart Alec's".

There were also men dancing bare footed on broken bottles, chewing broken glass into pulp and then swallowing it. Another man, stripped to the waist, would swallow a pocket watch on a long chain and invite a member of his audience to place an ear against his stomach to hear it ticking, and then withdraw it. Next, he would light a large flame torch and extinguish it by inserting it into the mouth and after a few seconds, opening his mouth, when a great billow of smoke would be released. Large crowds gathered to see this perverse form of entertainment and while it was being performed an accomplice was going round with a collecting box and it was not unknown for a few people to lose their wallets and other valuables.

The "cheap jacks" displayed a wide variety of goods on their stalls.

One had crockery and would set up a dinner service on the large dish and auction it off in the reverse order, starting at a high price and gradually reducing it until he reached what he termed "the rock bottom price" and then they usually went like "hot cakes". At the same time as he was extolling their high quality he would toss them a few feet into the air and after they came clattering down in his hands, would invite anyone to inspect them and if they discovered one piece broken, he would give them the whole service free.

A "Quack Doctor" would usually start his practice by dispatching a boy from the audience to purchase a long list of medical items from the local chemist shop and on return the boy received "tuppence" for the errand. Next, the doctor would ask the audience if they suffered from any complaint and having been told one, would mix up a concoction and hand it in a bottle, if in liquid form, or if in ointment form, in a small pillbox and charge from 1/- to 2/6, depending on the cost of the ingredients used. He would carry on making up the "wonderful secret mixture" as long as he could find a customer.

A typical example of a "Smart Alec" was the man with a suit case containing about 100 wage packets, each with a small priceless article inside. After a few rallying calls and a bit of banter to attract a large crowd he would start his business by informing the audience that each package contained a small, but useful gift. Then he would place a pocket watch in about twenty packets and a golden sovereign in five or six more and mix them in with those already filled in the case. Picking out one of the bulkier looking packets he would ask who would give him a shilling for it. Usually one of the first three customers found a watch in the packet, but the next twenty or so received useless articles. Then, as no more customers were forthcoming, he would place another sovereign in a packet and offer it to someone for 2/6, but by sleight of hand the packet, when opened, only contained another useless gift.

In the early 1920's the High Street, from Thetford Road to the brewery, would be packed solid with people by 11 a.m. until 6 p.m., when they would wind their way to the fair on Mr. Sample's meadow. A few years later there were other fairs on both Hall & Palmer's and Barnham's sale meadows and also a circus on what is now Lime Tree Walk. On wet days the fair grounds were soon inches deep in mud and dozens of people lost a boot or shoe in the gluey squelch. Undeterred they continued tramping from coconut and skittle stands, to boxing booths and rock stalls, remarking that they might as well get wet outside as in, having previously spent much of the day in one, or another, of the dozen inns in the town at that time.

*Lord Walsingham presenting the S. S. George Challenge Shield on Show Day to Rosemary Dennis for the best athlete in the school for 1948. Rosemary went on to run for the county and in the All England Championships.*
*Left to right: - Mr S. S. George, Lord Walsingham, Lt. Col Barnham, Mr Shepherd Page, Rosemary Dennis and Mr. H.J Rump.*

After the last war the character of the show changed completely with exceptionally large entries in both the horse jumping and goat classes. Dog competitions were also introduced and out went the fodder crops of mangels, swedes and turnips, while rabbits, poultry, sheep and pigs were also missing from many a "show day", but each year saw more and more commercial stands, many of which had no connection with agriculture.

The last forty years have seen vast social changes and with most families possessing a car, thus enabling them to find their entertainment further afield, fodder crops and the like wouldn't attract a single visitor to-day. The show organisers must find it more and more difficult to provide crowd-pulling entertainment each year and I am sure they would welcome any new idea's in this field, as without the income received from commercial stands etc., it would probably be impossible to make sufficient money to continue running the Wayland Show.

# THE MARKETS

*Cattle in Hall & Palmer's Sale Yard 1934.*

As mentioned in another chapter, Watton had five annual fairs for cattle and sheep for many generations and since 1870, and possibly much earlier, a cattle sale was held for several years at the rear of the "George Hotel" on alternate Wednesdays.

Hall & Palmer's started their weekly stock markets at their Norwich Road sale yard in 1902. Between the wars it became one of the largest cattle markets in the county apart from Norwich and King's Lynn. At their weekly sales it was not unusual for them to have 200 cattle and at the special monthly sales somewhere in the region of 400 cattle and 300 pigs would be penned with lesser numbers of sheep and a few horses. Throughout the year the weekly poultry sales attracted many hundreds of chickens and rabbits, with a dozen or two goats and guinea pigs. Large quantities of butter, eggs and vegetables were also auctioned.

The annual fat stock and poultry sales were the highlight of the year with the prize-winning bullocks fetching high prices and a week later their prime joints were displayed in the butcher's shops, together with their prize-winning cards.

Preparations for their Christmas Poultry Sale went on for a week or two before the auction day, with hundreds of temporary pens being erected on the large sale meadow to accommodate thousands of fat turkeys and geese and the permanent pens were filled with fat chickens.

Barnham's Stock sales started in the "Bull Hotel" yard in 1900 and they moved to the Norwich Road site, where Noel Abel now has his furniture sales, in 1912. They sold fewer cattle, but their entries of pigs were probably higher than Hall & Palmer's, while weekly numbers of chickens, eggs, butter and vegetables was usually well in access of Hall & Palmer's with some 20,000 to 25,000 eggs being handled each week.

Half a dozen Jews would come down on the train from London and competition between themselves and local buyer, George Page, was so keen that it provided much humorous entertainment with the likes of Grossmein and Honingstein gabbling away until the auctioneers gavel came down for the last lot. Then it was all hustle and bustle to get the fowls into crates and taken up to the station in time to catch the train for London.

With the outbreak of war these markets were taken over as collection centres by the Ministry of Agriculture with Mr. H. Palmer being appointed as the local supervisor. Hall & Palmer's were allotted the centre for cattle and Barnham's for pigs. By the time the collecting centres finished operating in 1955 both firms had considerably increased the other side of their business of Estate Agents, Valuers etc., and the cattle markets were not restarted.

In 1924 Lt. Col. Barnham erected the wooden building alongside the Norwich Road as a furniture Sale Room and for the next 40 years up to a thousand lots of furniture were auctioned there most Wednesdays. As well as being an auction room, it served the town as a hall where a wide variety of functions were held until the opening of the Queen's Hall in 1956. The "Sale Rooms" as they were known to everyone, have recently been converted into a branch of the Westminster Bank. Twelve years after leaving school and starting work for H. G. Barnham & Son as an auctioneers clerk, Noel Abel took over the business in its entirety on the retirement of Lt. Col. Barnham. In 1962-3 he had the present spacious auction rooms built on the site where some of the pig pens were previously situated.

*Part of Abel's Removal Complex on the Norwich Road.*

During the last few years the Market Stalls on Wednesdays have increased considerably. Before the last war they occupied both sides of Middle Street, the Market Place and along the High Street as far as the Clock Tower. Now there are none in Middle Street, but the Market Place is still full and they extend down to the old brewery along the north side of High Street with the odd one or two on the south side.

In addition to carrying on with the weekly furniture sales, Noel Abel and his son Tony have built up one of the largest removal and storage business in the country. In 1972 a large complex of storage and removal buildings were erected opposite the R.A.F. Station on the Norwich Road. These were considerably expanded in 1980 and now cover an area of 8 acres with a storage space of 54,000 square feet. A fleet of 61 removal vans, which include some of the largest removal vehicles allowed on British roads, make regular trips to Germany and other European countries as well as Singapore and Australia, thereby putting Watton very much on the map. One of the firms most important contracts was the removal of the effects of the Prince and Princess of Wales from Buckingham Palace to their home at Highgrove. Another of Abel's special assignments was moving an exhibition for the Sultan of Oman 6,000 miles across Europe. Mr. Paul Kryger drove the large removal van through Sweden, Denmark, Norway and Austria, stopping in towns and cities on the route to display the exhibition for His Majesty Sultan Oaboos bin Said, the Sultan. With a staff of 180, Abel's are now one of the largest employers of labour in the town.

*One of three removal vans at Buckingham Palace*

79

# IN WAYLAND WOOD
# THE BABES WERE FOUND

What have St. Mary's Church, Watton and Wayland Wood in common? Both are situated on the outskirts of the parish and whilst the former is the oldest building in the town, having served the residents for nearly 900 years, the latter has attracted Wattonians to view its extensive carpets of wood anemones, primroses and bluebells and to hear the delightful dawn chorus of its birds for over a thousand years. With the exception of Sherwood Forest and Selwood it is the oldest wood in England. It became nationally famous when legend linked it with the sinister deaths of the Babes in the Wood.

After the Saxon armies had won back the Danelaw about 950 they divided the reconquered land into Hundreds and wherever possible named them after some natural feature in the district. Thus it was that the area forming a rough triangle between Attleborough, East Harling and Watton, together with the surrounding villages were named the "Wayland Hundred". The Domesday Book refers to it as Wane-lond. As lond means wood it will be realised that Wayland Wood gave its name to the Hundred and not vice-versa. Various theories have been suggested as to how the legend of the Babes in the Wood came to be associated with Watton's Wayland Wood.

One of them is that the Elizabethan Manor House, standing a half mile to the south-east, contained—until about a hundred years ago—a carved over mantel of the period, depicting the story of the Babes, so even in Elizabeth l's time it was already a legend. It was also in this house that the Wicked Uncle, who paid two ruffians to dispose of the Babes, was supposed to have lived.

*This house, a half mile past Wayland Wood, is supposed to be where the "Wicked Uncle" lived.*

As all the world knows, the story of the Babes in the Wood has for hundreds of years been a favourite subject for Christmas pantomimes. From the 14th century until 1975 the wood was owned by the de Grey Family, but it was almost lost during Elizabethan times when Robert de Grey, a staunch Papist, who owned it at the time, was in Norwich gaol after having refused to attend the Anglican services, or to pay the fines incurred by his action. His estate was taken over by the Crown and let to racketeers known as Crown Lesses. Two of them, Thomas Felton and John Crotch, leased the wood and engaged a gang of men to fell it. But a friend of Robert de Grey's, Francis Woodhouse of Breckles, heard a whisper of their intentions and warned Robert so that he could do something about it.

This he did by paying his fines and bailing himself out. Coming to his nearby Merton estate he collected the employees together and armed with staves and long-handled forks they rushed to Wayland Wood and told Felton and Crotch what would happen to them and their men if the trees were cut down. Discreetly they withdrew.

Having known this wood all my life I can remember my father taking me to the keeper's cottage when I was about seven and asking the keeper if he would show us the tree under which the babes were reputed to have been found, buried by a robin covering them with leaves. He escorted us far into the wood and stopping by the stump of a large tree, informed us that this was where they died, the tree having been destroyed by lightning in August 1879. As we made our way back to the road I realised how difficult this would have been without our guide, with so many overgrown paths crisscrossing each other in all directions. At this time it was not unknown on shooting days for one of the beaters to get lost in the wood during the last "drive" of the day, with darkness falling fast. Occasionally it meant he had to wait until morning light to find his way out. This would not happen today, as one can hear the continuous roar of traffic passing along the road and head towards it. None the less 30 years ago, when "birding" in the wood with a naturalist friend, we came upon an elderly man whom I knew very well, but owing to his dishevelled appearance did not recognise at once. He had grown a beard, was painfully thin and obviously so weak he could hardly stand. Although he managed a slight movement of his lips, no sound was forthcoming and we realised he was in a very serious condition. Informing the police, we were surprised to learn that he had been missing for three weeks and that they had spent many hours searching for him.

As he lived alone, arrangements were made for him to be cared for in a Thetford home and when I saw him a month later he thanked me for saving his life. It appeared that he had strolled far into the wood one afternoon and was unable to find his way out again, but it was not certain if he had been there all the time.

*Wayland Wood where the "Babes" are supposed to have been buried.*

In 1975 Lord Walsingham decided to sell this 85 acres of deciduous woodland to the Norfolk Naturalist Trust for a very modest fee to ensure the conservation of its botanical character, its bird life, and not least, its long history.

For many centuries the wood was a productive asset and the large hazel stools produced pea sticks, bean and hop poles and thatcher's "broachers". Until recent years the Great Ouse River Authority also used to cut five acres each year for making "fascines", brushwood faggots, used in reclamation work in the marshy fenland areas. Today, the only folk making use of the hazelwood are the local thatchers, the Mindham family of Merton, who for generations have cut their 'broachers" in the wood. Lord Walsingham obtained an assurance from the Norfolk Naturalists Trust that they be allowed to continue before he sold it.

Today Wayland Wood contains few oak or ash trees of any considerable age, having contributed its finest timber to the wartime needs of the country on more than one occasion. Bird cherry beautifies the roadside during May, several tall sallows and maples, a few aspen and some really fine old hollies remain. In their season the wood is carpeted with white anemones, primroses and bluebells. Also large patches of yellow archangel, bugle, water avens, alkanet and various orchids. Botanically however, it is most famous as the only known place in Norfolk where the yellow star of Bethlehem grows, attracting botanists from far and wide. The usual woodland birds are to be found, including all three species of British woodpeckers, treecreepers, nuthatch, woodcock, owls, tits and warblers. Some years the rich song of the nightingale was much in evidence, while in others not more than two pairs were present. They have declined considerably in recent years and I have not heard one there for a long time.

# THE BAND

Official records show that Watton has had a band for over a century and one may well have been in existence long before then as there is mention of a band playing at various functions in the town from the early 1700's, but it does not state if it was a Watton band, or one visiting the town.

*Watton Town Band 1932*

In 1890 it was known as "The Volunteer Band", but before the turn of the century it became the Watton Town Band and as such won its first band competitions. By the early 1930's it became the Watton

British Legion Band for about twenty years when it again changed to its present title of Watton and District Band. In April 1950 there was great jubilation when they won their first ever major prize, the Class 'C' Contest at the East Anglian Brass Band Association Festival, also the Reepham and the Sir Thomas Cook Challenge Cups. More success followed in 1955 by winning the Class 'B' Contest.

Their greatest achievements however were in 1966, 1969 and 1976 when they won the Class 'A' Contests at the East Anglian Brass Band Association Festivals thus gaining entrance into the Championship Section. Since gaining their first major contest the band has secured many engagements all over the county including Great Yarmouth, Hunstanton and in the Norwich Parks. For several years there were five members of one family in the band, Jimmy Woods and his sons, Victor, George, Allen and Cyril, while another son Harold, played in a local Dance Band.

Since those great years many of the older members have retired, but several young bandsmen are now coming along nicely under the tuition of John Whalebelly who is always on the look out for keen musicians to join them.

# THE COTTAGE HOSPITAL

In 1897, £700 was raised by public subscription to build a Cottage Hospital on a site made available by Lord Walsingham on the Thetford Road. It was officially opened in July 1899 and named "The Victoria Cottage Hospital" to commemorate the Diamond Jubilee of Queen Victoria. An operating theatre was added in 1904 and in 1907 a children's ward was built at a cost of £200 and the building programme was completed in 1933 when a new wing was added. During the fifty or so years of its existence it was extensively used for minor ailments, accident and maternity cases and at the annual meeting in March 1947 it was reported that the number of patients for 1946 was 1,032.

Following the formation of the National Health Service it was closed on February 9th 1950, but the feeling in the town was that it should have stayed open, as not only would it have been an asset to local residents, but would have helped to relieve the waiting list at the Norwich Hospitals. Thus in July 1951 members of the East Anglian Regional Hospital Board and the Senior Administrative Medical Officer met local representatives to discuss the hospital's future and the outcome of this meeting was that it should remain closed.

*Watton Cottage Hospital in the late 1920s.*

In November the same year the Parish Council asked Mr. P. Baker, the M.P., for his help to secure its re-opening, but he was unable to persuade the Hospital Board to reconsider their decision. It was later sold and converted into flats and bungalows were erected in its pleasant grounds and this development is now known as Victoria Court. Much hard work was put into various efforts to raise the necessary money to keep the hospital running. Whist drives, dances, in fact an endless list of events were organised, with perhaps the two best remembered being the Annual Watton Hospital Cup in which many local football clubs competed over the years and the annual Hospital Carnival Weeks that started in 1927.

My first recollection of the Hospital Cup matches was in the 1919-20 season when Thetford Town, then one of the best teams in Norfolk, Brandon, Diss, Swaffham and Wymondham were among the many competitors. These matches were played on the grounds of the teams drawn first out of the hat and my father took me with him in Mr. R. G. Holmes's car, who at that time was the competition secretary, to see Watton lose at Thetford. A year or two later Hingham upset the form book by beating Thetford 2-1 in the final, which was always played at Watton

*The 1934 Carnival Queen and her attendants.*
*Left to right: - Frances Edwards, Jose Rust, Joyce Bird, Doreen Whalebelly, Joan Turgoose, Dawn Eyre and Marion Spinks.*
*Doreen was the first Carnival Queen to be elected by public vote.*

A few years later it was decided to limit the number of teams to four with all the matches being played at Watton, with Ashill, Rockland, Shipdham, Hockham, Hingham and Great Cressingham being among the teams invited to participate over the years. This created much more local interest and proved a great success with the Final attracting crowds of over 2,000. When Ashill were in the Final, just about everyone from the village came to cheer them which created an electrical atmosphere and win, or lose, the sportsmanship of all teams and supporters in those days was exemplary. Like Watton Show Day, the Hospital Carnival Weeks were looked forward to from one year to the next and what wonderful social occasions they were, with something for everyone to partake in. Sundays were devoted to Sacred Concerts and United Services and on Mondays the Carnival Queen was crowned at Loch Neaton. Previous to 1934 the Carnival Queen's were selected by the committee, but from then on they were elected by public vote.

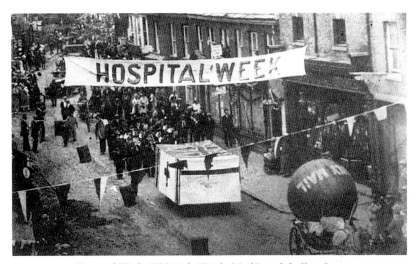

*Hospital Week 1929 with "Daily Mail" push ball in front.*

Bowls, tennis and swimming competitions were the main events at the Loch on Monday evenings. A variety concert, or a musical revue was the usual Tuesday fare. Throughout Wednesday's there was 'A Trail of Pennies", when thousands were laid along the kerb of the main streets and in the evening "A Mystery Treasure Hunt" was followed by a Grand Dance. Thursday was "The Great Day" with a "Monster Carnival Procession" up to two miles long, followed by various entertainments on a meadow that is now part of Charles Avenue. Probably the best remembered were Watts Naval Training School Display Party and the Internationally Famous Dagenham Girl Pipers, and both these groups also provided a band that together with our own British Legion Band, escorted the Carnival Procession around the town. Friday was usually taken up with a Non-stop Whist Drive and Saturday was another marvellous day with Rodeo acts, motor cycle gymkhana's etc., after which the week concluded with another "Grand Carnival Dance".

Following the closure of the hospital various organisations have carried on running a Carnival Week and raising considerable sums of money that have benefited many worthy causes including the British Legion, R.A.F. Benevolent Fund, Silver Thread Club, Watton and District Band, Loch Neaton Swimming Pool, Children's Playground Equipment, Memorial Playing Field, F.E.P.O.W. Association, Youth Centre, Watton Sports Association and the Boy Scouts.

# THE R.A.F. STATION

There can be no doubt that September 1936 saw the beginning of a great new era for Watton, for it was during this month that a start was made on the construction of the R.A.F. Station. The preliminary work of purchasing the site, which took in part of the villages of Carbrooke and Griston, as well as Watton had been completed and surveying work carried out.

Many agricultural workers who were on a lower wage rate than their industrial counterparts were quick to grasp this opportunity of improving their standard of living. The first manual work was not unlike what some of them had occasionally carried out on the farms, felling trees, removing hedges, piping and filling in ditches. Having cleared the area where the four large hangars were to be built a start was made on excavating the holes that were to take the huge iron stanchions which comprised part of the vast framework of the hangars. Surprisingly, these holes which were about 12 feet by 8 and about 7 feet deep were all dug out by hand labour and thus those workers who left the farms were able to transfer from agricultural to industrial work gradually and although the work was sometimes harder, this was compensated with a bulkier wage packet each week. The next three years saw a dramatic transformation of the site as first the hangars came into being to be followed by the Station HO., Guard Room, Hospital, Officers, Sergeants and Airmen's messes, living quarters and a hundred and one other buildings that went into the completion of the station. With large numbers of specialists craftsmen from far-a-field now living in the town and others being brought in from nearby towns and villages daily, trade in the town started to boom. Gone forever were the days when everyone knew everyone else and if a stranger was spotted he, or she, was almost certainly a holiday-maker. Now it was different, strangers were no longer holiday makers, but "workers on the camp". The building work was sufficiently advanced for the station to be opened on 4th January, 1939 under Group Capt. F. J. Vincent. Officers and airmen and their families moved into married quarters and planes began to appear around the hangars and soon the throb of their engines became a familiar sound.

3rd, September 1939, was a grave day, not only for Watton, but for the whole country, as at 11 a.m. war was declared. At the outbreak of war two squadrons of Blenheim Bombers, No's 21 and 82 formed No. 79 wing and made photographic reconnaissance of the north German ports and over the North Sea. After Dunkirk, the most active part of R.A.F. Watton's history followed with their attacks being directed against targets in France and Belgium, the invasion ports and targets in Germany. Losses of airmen and aircraft were heavy and on two occasions in 1940 No. 82 Squadron lost 11 out of 12 Blenheims despatched on day-light raids and it was not until mid 1941 that fighter escorts became available for day-light operations. Many heroic acts were performed by the R.A.F. from our local station and it is to be hoped that both present and all future Wattonians will remember those who lost their lives from this station with pride and thanksgiving.

Operations continued throughout 1941 and into 1942 against shipping and airfields and in October 1942 No. 82 Squadron was transferred to the Middle East. Early in 1942 Bomber Command relinquished control of Watton and for sixteen months it was used by No. 17 Advanced Flying Unit, training pilots on advanced flying techniques and instrument flying. Among No. 82 Squadron's Commanders were the Earl of Bandon and Sir Charles Elsworthy who was decorated three times during his stay at Watton with the D.S.O., D.F.C. and A.F.C.

With the massive build up of the American Eighth Air Force it soon became apparent that large servicing Units would be needed to cope with the tremendous task of maintaining aircraft at war. It was decided to set up four such units to be known as Strategic Air Depots (S.A.D.) and the 3rd S.A.D. was established at R.A.F. Watton.

The first American airmen arrived at the Station on 23rd July 1943. Their job was to maintain, service, repair and carry out modifications on all the aircraft in the second Air Division. It was the second Air Division who occupied 14 bases in Norfolk, flying B24 Liberators. At the height of operations 6,600 American personnel were at Watton. This was about three times the town's population at this time.

A large complex was built on the Griston side of the Airfield and work went on night and day to keep the B24's flying. It has been said that the 3rd S.A.D. knew more about the B24's than did the Consolidated Aircraft Co., who manufactured them, and when reading of their exploits, this is quite believable. A telegraph pole was once used to strengthen the fragile fuselage of a Liberator, enabling it to be flown from Shipdham to Watton for repairs.

*"Pistol Packing Mama" outside a Watton hangar, awaiting repairs, Jan. 1st 1944.*

*The "Urgin Virgin" was the first Liberator to be repaired at Watton RAE Station by the American Air Force. Note how the Americans painted a striking picture on their aircraft, 1943 in one of the hangars.*

On 22nd April 1944 the 25th Bomb Group arrived under the command of Col. Eliot Roosevelt, son of the American President, Franklyn D. Roosevelt. It was a unique group in that they flew the British Mosquitos. The men who flew with the 25th had already completed a tour of 35 combat missions and had volunteered to fly with the 25th B.G. The Mosquitos were completely unarmed which enabled them to fly faster and higher than other aircraft. They were involved in weather reconnaissance, photographic reconnaissance, pathfinding and espionage missions. The 25th also flew a few B17's on weather reconnaissance. A very well kept secret was the presence of the "Black Liberators" ("The Carpet-baggers") who flew top secret espionage missions. The 25th B.C. left Watton on 23rd July 1945 and the 3rd S.A.D. on 5th August 1945. The 25th Bomb Group lost about 70 airmen and the repair unit just one, a Chaplain who volunteered for work in France and was killed in a Jeep accident. In June 1984 fifty former U.S. Airmen returned to Watton R.A.F. for the unveiling of a most beautiful Memorial situated just inside the Main Gates.

*This Memorial to the U.S.A.A.F. 25th Bomb Group (RCN. SP.) can be seen just inside the Main Gates at Watton R.A.F. Station.*

The Station re-opened late in 1945 as the Radio Warfare Establishment and in 1946 this became the Central Signals Establishment. In October 1965 Eastern Radar was established and came into operation as a parented Unit adjacent to the Station. It is functionally and operationally controlled by NATO and gives radar control and surveillance to all aircraft flying over East Anglia. The news that the R.A.F. was to be run down at the end of 1969 came as a bombshell to the town, especially as it was feared that about 250 civilian jobs would be lost and the customer potential of the town's shops could be reduced by fifty per cent.

Today part of the station is occupied by the Honington R.A.F. Admin. Wing Detachment, but sadly many of the houses and buildings are unoccupied. Army personnel from the nearby Stanford Battle Area make use of the airfield for training purposes while the airmen's mess on the opposite side of the road to the main camp has been sold and is used as industrial units.

I never pass the Main Gates without reflecting on my school days, as for many years my father farmed the fields where many of the important buildings were erected, including the Station Head Quarters, Guard Room, Hospital, Sergeant's Mess and Air Ministry Offices. Many a time I have gone home very tired after planting potatoes all day, helping with the harvest and, like most boys in those days, thought it great fun chasing rabbits as they bolted for the safety of the hedges when the last few strips of corn were about to be cut.

# THE QUEEN'S HALL

In October 1952 Watton Parish Council called a meeting to consider what would form a suitable commemoration of the Coronation of Her Majesty Queen Elizabeth II. A large majority favoured the erection of a Public Hall as there was a long standing need for such an amenity in Watton. A committee was appointed and quickly embarked on their formidable task of providing a Public Hall and the subsidiary task of organising Coronation Festivities in the town.

Within a year a suitable site had been purchased and the idea of using an existing steel hangar frame as the mainstay of the building was adopted and negotiations for such a frame commenced. A hangar was purchased on December 29th 1953 and in three weeks was dismantled and brought to Watton for cleaning and painting. Plans for the Hall having been approved by all the authorities concerned, the boundary wall, fronting Norwich Road, was breached and an entrance cut to the site on April 5th 1954.

Work on felling 18 trees, bulldozing out roots and excavating for building foundations proceeded rapidly and by August 1954 the hangar frame was erected. Having complied with the necessary conditions for obtaining a Ministry of Education grant, notification was received from the Ministry during September that a grant of £1,762 would be paid by installments, providing that the work was done by voluntary labour.

Electricity was installed and work proceeded under floodlights during the winter of 1954-55 and by June 1955 the walls were up to window level and in July the building was roofed. Work was carried out inside the hall during the next winter and by January the concrete roof over the entrance hall and balcony was completed and the stage and ceiling joists fixed. A month later the ceiling was finished, the walls plastered and plans made to open the Hall on November 1st 1956.

During April, May and June the sprung dance floor, balcony and staircase was proceeded with and connection made with the public sewage system, thereby completing the main features of the construction programme. From July on many smaller jobs were carried out to ensure a reasonable state of completion by November 1st.

In completing this exceptionally fine hall, which measures 105 feet in length by 36 feet in width, the original committee and everyone who gave their time and money, both during its erection and in maintaining it since, are to be congratulated and everyone in the town and district owe them a great debt of gratitude.

So Watton's new Queen's Hall was officially opened on 1st November 1956 by Lady Bacon who was accompanied by her husband, Sir Edmund, the Lord Lieutenant of Norfolk.

For the ten days following the opening of the Hall a great variety of events took place, both in the hall and in and around the town, including dances, band and choral concerts, a torchlight procession and firework party, plays, whist drives and talent competitions.

The original committee were Mr. V. P. Alderton, Mr. R. G. Durrant, Mr. and Mrs. J. B. Fairhead, Mrs. J. Farrall, Mr. F. C. Fitt, Mr. W. J. Horne, Mr. J. W. Kittell, Mr. and Mrs. G. Shepherd Page, Mr. L. J. Saward and Mr. L. Watling. Later Miss E. T. Cracknell, Mr. R. B. Nunn and Mr. B. Sharman were co-opted.

*Mr R. Durrant speaking at the opening of the Queen's Hall by Sir. Edmund Bacon O.B.E. on Nov. 1st 1956.*

# WATTON MEMORIAL PLAYING FIELD

The Primary object of the Playing Fields was to perpetuate the names of those who gave their lives in the Second World War. The Secondary object was to provide playing fields to be named the "Watton Memorial Playing Fields" to cater for all classes of outdoor sport. Originally nine acres of land were to be purchased that had been zoned as Playing

Fields by the Planning Authorities. In July 1947 a house to house collection was arranged and the towns-people asked to subscribe generously, as the estimated cost of buying and equipping the site was £3,000, a very large sum in those days. But these were times of austerity with food still in short supply following five years of war. Many snags were therefore encountered before the land was finally released by the agricultural committee and with prices rising steeply all the time, it appeared at one stage that the project would be a very long while before it materialised.

A committee was formed in the late 1950's, headed by Frank Dye, Sen., and first a site of six acres was purchased, levelled, drained and seeded and with the help of much voluntary work the first part of the sports field was eventually opened in 1961. It consisted of a full size football pitch, cricket square and outfield, hard-based practice nets, hockey pitch, two tennis courts and a children's play area. Before matches could be played, changing facilities had to be erected and the football club purchased an "Arcon" hut for £450 which was erected, fitted out with changing rooms and decorated throughout and a further £200 was spent on baths and showers etc. The view from the sports field across the valley to Ovington and Saham Toney, with its Church in the background, is one of breathtaking beauty on a fine summer evening, but during the winter the football supporters soon realised that the north wind sweeping across the open space chilled the spine and soon a party of volunteers were working like beavers in erecting a stand on the north side of the pitch.

After a few years Mr. Dick Durrant and Mr. Dudley Bowes generously provided another acre or so and a further nine acres was purchased by the town council. This enabled the hockey pitch to be resited, two junior football pitches to be laid out, a full size E.B.A. Bowling Green to be created and a large extension added to the car park. During the summer of 1984 Floodlights were erected at each corner of the football pitch, thus giving many more supporters the opportunity to watch football, who otherwise, due to their working hours, would never have the chance of seeing the team play.

In March this year, Ian Botham, one of the world's greatest cricketers, who also plays football for Scunthorpe United in the Football League, brought along an All Star Xl to play Watton to raise some money towards the £22,000 needed to pay for the lights, The game was arranged by Bob Oates, who took over as manager of the Sports Centre when Tom Pettitt retired after nearly ten years dedicated service. Bob was a team mate of Ian's at Scunthorpe.

On Tuesday, 30th April 1985, the largest crowd to watch a match on this ground saw Watton excel themselves to beat a Norwich City team 1-0 that included five of the side who had recently won the Milk Cup at Wembley. During the evening Mick Channon, the English International officially opened the Floodlights.

*The Memorial Sports Field showing the Floodlights erected in 1984 and Officially opened by Mick Channon on April 30th 1985.*

# WATTON SPORTS CENTRE

*Watton Sports Centre built between 1973 and 1984.*

In August 1968 a meeting of representatives of the various sports clubs in the town was held and agreed to go ahead with the idea of building a Sports Centre for the town, which was the idea of Ken Worden, the secretary of Watton United Football Club. As a result of this meeting the Sports Association was formed under the chairmanship of Noel Dye who sent out a circular appealing for donations and within a half hour the first donation was pushed through his door by Mrs. Bantick who lived nearby. After five years of fund raising events she was invited to cut the first turf on April 8th 1973, to get the first stage of what was to become a vast sports complex, under way.

Included in the first phase were the main games hall with badminton court, lounge bar area, committee rooms, full-sized snooker table, kitchen, changing rooms, bath and shower facilities, storage space, outside balcony, car park and some landscaping work.

The original estimated cost of this phase was £13,000, but due to inflation the final figure was a staggering £35,000 of which grants amounting to £7,000 have been received with the rest being raised by local efforts. At the same time it was hoped to complete the shell of the second stage, which would include two squash courts, a meeting room and hall combined, and additional changing accommodation and showers, for which another estimated £22,000 would have to be raised.

Saturday 14th September 1974 saw the Official Opening of the first stage of Wattons Sports Centre by Sir Edmund Bacon, Lord Lieutenant of Norfolk and it was a just reward for the officers of the Sports Association and all who supported them by their hard work, endeavour and encouragement.

Within two years the second stage had been completed and this was officially opened by the Rt. Hon. Lord Luke KC, VO, TD, DL, Chairman of the National Playing Fields Association. With the first two phases now in operation, the chairman and committee had every right to be proud of their achievements and the most important and encouraging factor was that the centre was already being extremely well used, with more and more of the general public joining and considering it to be their club. This certainly convinced the officials that there was a great need for such sporting facilities in the town as they were providing.

During the next few years, work on the third phase continued to go ahead steadily and on 23rd July 1982 Mr. Dick Jeeps, CBE, the Chairman of the Sports Council officially opened the third stage of Watton's Sports Centre which cost £80,000 and was paid for from profits from the existing sections of the centre that had been ploughed back into a fund for future development. He also unveiled a plaque built into the outside of the main building which had been donated by the local stonemason, Alan Blake. The new addition will provide facilities for five-a-side football, cricket nets, badminton and basketball and covers an area of 80 feet by 45 feet. An extension to the snooker room has enabled another table to be installed and at the time of writing a new committee room and additional toilet facilities are in the course of construction

Over the years various money raising events have been organised and the thanks of everyone using the facilities at the centre are due to all who helped in any way. From the outset the major source of money raising was the forming of a "100" club, which was soon fully subscribed. It then became a "200" club and has now peaked at "500". The initial success of the "Draw Club" was ensured by the hard work of its first secretary, Jane Dye; and the untiring efforts of Eileen Ward, the present secretary, has seen a continuation of that success.

# SPORT

# BOWLS

Over the years Watton has been to the forefront of many sporting activities. Bowls is the oldest sport recorded in the town and as far back as 1681 a visitor to the town mentioned a fine new bowling green at the "George Hotel".

When Loch Neaton pleasure grounds were created in 1892 a bowling green was incorporated in the lay-out and games between townsmen were played from that time. But it was not until 3rd, April 1900 that the Loch Neaton Bowls Club was officially formed and from that year friendly matches were played against other local clubs. One of them being the Watton Liberal Bowling Club, whose green was on the site of the new International Stores.

The first County Championship honours to be won by members of the Loch Club was in 1931 when E. Doyle, E. A. Adcock and F. W. Saunders won the Norfolk Triples. League matches were first played in 1947 when the club entered both the South Norfolk and Wymondham and District Leagues, winning the former at the first attempt and again in 1949 and 1950. In 1955 they won both the Dereham & District League and the Norfolk & Suffolk Border Shield.

In 1956 C. A. Saunders, W. A. Porter and R. Cogle were chosen to play for Norfolk for the first of many occasions. The same year C. A. Saunders became Norfolk County E.B.A. Singles Champion and in 1957 he was the Yarmouth Open Bowls Champion. E. Gunson was also chosen to play for Norfolk in 1957.

1958 brought more success for the Loch bowlers when C. A. Saunders and J. Farrall won the Norfolk County E.B.F. Pairs Championship and represented Norfolk in the E.B.F. Championships at Skegness. They repeated this feat again in 1964 and in the same season were losing finalists in the Norfolk A.B.A. Pairs Championship. In 1966 E. Gunson won the Norfolk County E.B.A. Singles Championship.

After 90 years bowling on Loch Neaton's "Green" the Club was disbanded in 1982 as a new Bowling Green had been constructed during the previous two years on the adjoining War Memorial Playing Field and most of the Loch Neaton Club Members transferred to the new Watton Town Bowls Club.

1936 saw the birth of another Watton bowls club, the "Bull Hotel" and they also had a number of successes before finishing in 1970. Three of their members, E. Haines, J. Lucas and E. Gunson won the Norfolk County E.B.F. Triples Championship in 1967.

*Loch Neaton Bowls Club circa 1895.*
*Sitting, from the left: S. Short, Sheperd Howlett, Win. Whalebelly. The two gents in*
*"boaters" are Teddy Toombs and Thomas Tennant. Two of the boys at the front are*
*Teddy Toombs's sons.*

*Loch Neaton Bowls Club 1932. How many can you name?*

*Christmas Day Bowls.*

*The "Bull Hotel" Bowls Club.*

# FOOTBALL

The first mention of a football team in Watton was in 1888 and the first photographic record is for the 1896-7 season when several distinguished players donned the Watton colours. Although they had many fine teams over the years, they don't appear to have been in any league until after the first world war when they entered the Dereham & District League, winning it on a number of occasions in the 1920's and their best pre-war season was 1926-7 when they won the League, the Wilson Peace Cup and the Watton Hospital Cup. In 1951 Watton United won the Championship of Div. II of the East Anglian League and both the Swaffham and Watton Charity Cups and in 1953 and 1967 they won the Anglian Combination League Cup.

*Watton Football Team, Season 1896-7. Left to right*
*Back row, left to right: ———, L. Vincent, A. Howlett, —, A. Bailey, F.Adcock.*
*Middle row: P. Vincent, ———, S. Vincent, L. Julnes, F. Jessup. Front row: ———,*
*A. Julnes.*

The following players have been selected to play for Norfolk on a number of occasions. John Saunders in 1967, Chris Warner 1968 and Bob Oates, Mark Allcock, Karl Bristow and Mick Patterson in 1985. Ken Worden, who was the club secretary for thirty years, and also one of their most prolific goal scorers, gained his Suffolk County Colours when playing for Lowestoft Town. He remained secretary of Watton during his short playing career at Lowestoft and returned to add to his impressive goal-scoring feats. Undoubtedly the finest season Watton United have ever had was 1966-7 when the first Xl, the reserves and the "A" team won 8 out of the 9 competitions they entered. The Norfolk Senior Cup being the only trophy they failed to win, losing by the odd goal to C.N.S.O.B. in the semi-final. This trophy has still eluded them, the nearest they have been to winning it was in 1971 when Fakenham beat them 2-0 in the final at Carrow Road. From 1900 to the first world war Watton had another fine team, the Liberal Club, who played friendly matches against some of the best teams in Norfolk at that time and the following report of a match against Yarmouth Garrison Artillery will interest some senior citizens who will remember most of those players: This match, played at Watton on the 20th was a splendid game ending 1-1. Swann in the Watton goal was particularly brilliant. The Watton team was, Swann, Doyle and McEwen, Harvey H., Tennant and Nice, Myhill, Farrall A., Pickering, Carter and Drake. The Watton President thanked Yarmouth for giving them such a good game and said, "what a good season Watton were having, played 26, won 23, lost 2 and now drawn one. In fact, our team stands out as about the best small town team in the county". This game was played in March circa 1909.

*Watton Church Lads Football Club 1916-17*
*Back row, left to right: C. Rose, L. Brown, R. Davey, P. Fisher, K. Sturman,*
*A. Dunnett.*
*Front row: F. Lancaster, F. Hoy, J. Bedford, V. Tennant and D. Moore.*

During the First World War Watton Church Lads kept the flag flying and had some fine young players. During the 1930's Watton also had a Thursday team, but were unable to win the strong Norwich Thursday League in which they competed, usually finishing mid-way. During the 1960's and 70's Watton had a successful Sunday F.C. who won the Ouse Valley Sunday League and were twice losing finalists in the Norfolk Sunday Cup at Carrow Road, losing 5-1 to Earlham United in 1964 and 3-0 to Loke United in 1967. However, in 1977 they won the treble, winning the Thetford Sunday League, the League Knock-Out Cup and the Norfolk Sunday Junior Cup. The last season was also a good one for Watton United when they finished level on points with Wroxham who won the Anglian Combination Premier Division by only a two goal margin.

Congratulations to Watton Schoolboys under 13 football team on winning 8 trophies this season. Providing these lads can get employment locally when they leave school, the future for Watton United F.C. looks very bright.

*Watton United Football Club 1926-7 Season.*
*Back row, left to right: N. Peeke-vout, L. Adcock, J. Codling, K. Sturman, W. Hall, J. Gibb, F. Hoy, F. Head, E. Haines, G. Drake, S. Wyer, G. Jessup. Front row: R. Preston, T. Bedford, J. Farrall, G. Peachment (Capt.), A. Large and C. Rudd.*

*Watton United Football Club, Season 1967-8.*
*Front row: 1st XI, middle row: Reserves, back row: The 'A' Team,*
*front: The Goalkeepers.*

*In Season 1967-8 Watton United won 8 out of the 9 competitions they entered, these*
*are the trophy's*

# CRICKET

Just when Watton's first cricket club was formed is uncertain, but the first mention of cricket I could find was for 1845 when the town was reputed to have one of the finest cricket grounds in the country and this was situated behind the Bull Hotel, so it would appear that Watton possessed a cricket team some time before that date and one would assume that with a first class ground to play on, they would also have had a first class team. The first photographic record of a Watton cricket team is about 1890 and includes three players I well remember. Although Watton undoubtedly had some fine cricketers over the years they don't appear to have reached such a high team standard as the football teams and the only two records of a Watton cricketer being selected for Norfolk that I can trace were Edward Peachment in the 1920's and Andy Agar in 1982. In addition to the town club, the Liberal Club also ran a cricket team before the First World War

# SWIMMING

From the time Loch Neaton pleasure grounds were created in 1892, Watton has had a good swimming club. Each summer from its inception until the late 30's, Loch Neaton was the only local place one could go for swimming. Here water regattas and swimming competitions attracted large crowds with the "Buscall Shield" being the most coveted trophy for swimmers. Large crowds were provided with much fun from such events as "walking the greasy pole", pillow fighting with the competitors sitting astride the pole over the water, which often ended with both falling into the water together.

# TENNIS

Between the wars tennis enthusiasts were well catered for in the town and in addition to five or six private courts the Methodist Tennis Club had two grass courts next to the grounds of Harvey House and there were four public courts at Loch Neaton. Mrs. Robinson, wife of Charles the solicitor, won county honours for Norfolk and Tom Bedford and Lily Abbey, later becoming husband and wife, won practically all the local tournaments. Their daughter Pat holds the honour of being the only Watton player to partake in the Wimbledon tournaments, reaching the second round of the Junior Wimbledon in 1951.

*Watton Cricket Club 1934.*
*Back row, left to right: R. Watson, F. Haines, T. Page, J. Gibb, H. Battersby,*
*R. Upcher, P. Platten, A. Farrall. Front row: F. Knott, K. Carpenter, F. Harris.*

*Watton Hockey Club 1926.*
*Back row, left to right: C. Frazer, H. Adcock, F. Gunson, M. Banham, H. Newton,*
*W Harvey, Brand.*
*Front row: R. Adcock, F. Hill, C. Preston, B. Goss, B. Bullen.*

# THE MINIATURE RIFLE CLUB

The Watton Miniature Rifle Club was formed about 1900 and was in existence until around 1925. Their headquarters was at the Liberal Club and they were considered to be one of the best rifle clubs in the county—as confirmed in the "Thetford and Watton Post" dated 12th July 1906 which reads— "Talking of Cups, it was great to hear that Messrs E. Hendry, F. Jessup, A. Sayer and E. Tombs, members of Watton Rifle Club, have actually collared the Astor Cup for Norfolk this year. Fancy Watton having the honour of possessing the crack rifle club of the county". After the Liberal Club was disbanded in the mid 1920's the building was taken over by Wilfred Lane & Co., who were house furnishers and dealers in antiques, china and glass. A few years later Horace Siggins bought it for a butcher's shop and in the early 1950's it became the Ashill Meat Co.'s premises and in the mid 1950's Dudley Bowes started his Breckland Butchers business here. Later it became Codling's Shoe Shop until it was demolished to make way for the new Chemist Shop two years ago.

*Wayland Minature Rifle Club, Watton 1906. Teddy Toombs sitting in centre front row.*

# BOXING

Watton & District Amateur Boxing Club was formed in January 1970 under the guidance of Gordon Holmes, assisted by John Culyer and Arthur Bayliss. The club was fortunate to have many sponsors in its early days, including Henry Martineau of Saham Toney Hall, one of the countries leading livestock breeders, hence the club's emblem of a "Bull's Head". Many other local businessmen gave the club their support including Dudley and Kevin Bowes, both past presidents, Ted Riches, the late Eric Ogden and D. McDonald. Their first headquarters was in the former British Legion Hall, later they were granted the use of the Youth Club gymnasium until 1984, when they were fortunate in being offered the use of the fine Boxing Gymnasium at the R.A.F. Station, by kind permission of the C.O. Over the years the club has had many coaches and following his successful career with Watton A.B.C., Neil Brown was appointed chief coach in 1982 with Adrian Morley and Barry Trainer (Sen.), a former triple A.B.A. Champion, as assistants.

During its 15 years existence the club has had a remarkable list of achievements that include 33 Norfolk Champions, 22 Eastern Counties/Regional Champions, 7 National Quarter Finalists, 4 National Semi-finalists and 3 National Finalists. The following are among the most notable; —

1970  Peter Cox, Eastern Counties Senior Middleweight Champion.
David Holmes, National Schools Semi-Finalist.

1971  Peter Cox, Eastern Counties Senior Middleweight Champion.
Adrian Morley, Eastern Counties Senior Welterweight Champion.
David Holmes, Eastern Regional Schools Champion.

1972  Terry Stone, Eastern Counties Junior Champion.

1973  Neil Brown, Eastern Counties Junior Champion.

1974  Neil Brown, Norfolk Junior Champion.

1975  Neil Brown, Eastern Counties Senior Featherweight Champion.
Tony Whitmore, Eastern Counties Senior Bantamweight Champion and National A.B.A. Quarter Finalist.

1976 Tony Whitmore, Eastern Counties Senior Featherweight Champion and National A.B.A. Quarter Finalist.
Justin Fashanu, Eastern Counties Schools Champion and National Schools Finalist.

1977 Justin Fashanu, Eastern Counties Junior Champon and National Junior A.B.A. Finalist.

1979 Gary Champion, Norfolk, Eastern Counties and National Junior Semi-finalist.

1980 Michael Betts, Eastern Counties Junior Champion. Kenny Mudd, Eastern Counties Junior Champion.

1984 David Lawrence, Norfolk Light Heavyweight Chamnpion.

1985 Tony Lawrence, Eastern Counties Middleweight Champion.
Barry Trainer (Jun.) Eastern Counties Junior Champion and National Junior Finalist.

# CAR RACING

In 1971-2 Ted Savory was the East Anglian Saloon Car Champion, driving a specially prepared Ford Capri and setting several lap records in the process. Initially he started motor racing by way of Go-karting and he was in the England Kart team in 1962-3.

# THE CINEMAS

Like most children of my generation we experienced the excitement of our first visit to a cinema in 1919. At Watton it was a long wooden building situated between the vicarage grounds and Betty Hogg's Lane, now known as Priory Road.

These were the days of the "Slapstick Comedies" with Charlie Chaplin starring in "The Tramp", "The Goldrush" and "The Kid", etc. The black and white picture would appear on the screen to be followed by the words, which usually someone sitting near you read out aloud, thus saving you the effort. Breakdowns were frequent and one could usually anticipate them as they were generally preceded by much flickering. During the period when the fault was being repaired, Ella Rose, who entertained on the piano before the start, would be pressed into playing some of the popular tunes of the day, mostly old war time favourites like, "It's a long way to Tipperary", and everyone would join in.

Joe Swann, the projectionist, operated from a small compartment suspended from the roof of the building and the ladder used to gain access was then pushed back flush to the wall when he was inside so it should not impede people's view. One night his young assistant, Jack Roberts, stepped out of the projection room to come down the ladder and not realising it had been pushed back against the wall, he crashed to the floor, breaking his collar bone. After the cinema closed down, travelling concert parties used the building occasionally, usually staying a week, or two, at a time.

After that it became derelict for many years until the British Legion bought it and after renovation, used it as their HO. until it was demolished to make way for residential development about twelve years ago.

The first talking pictures to be shown in the town were at the Wayland Hall in the early 1930's and in 1938 the first purpose built cinema was opened on Norwich Road. For the next twenty years the "Regal" usually had a full house, but with television becoming increasingly popular the cinema audiences gradually became smaller and it finally closed down in March 1973.

Today the building is used by Richard Neave Ltd., International Movers and Storers. In the early days of the last war the Church Army built a large canteen on land adjoining the cinema for the use of service personnel and this was staffed by voluntary workers under the supervision of a Church Army Captain. Shortly after the war it was run down and the buildings were purchased by Messrs Harmer's in 1956 and converted into a clothing factory, closing down in April 1982 with the loss of 57 jobs. Once again it was sold and is now used by the Wayland Billiard and Snooker club.

*Richard Neave's removal vans outside their offices, the former 'Regal" Cinema.*

# THE RED CROSS DETACHMENT

The Watton Detachment of the Red Cross was formed in October 1931 with Mrs. Boag as Commandant. She was succeeded by Miss Blomfield who was Commandant for over 30 years. Following three emergencies in the town early in 1943 when there was no ambulance available to convey the patients to the Norwich Hospital, Miss Blomfield asked the County Authorities if an ambulance could be stationed at Watton. Being informed that there was no chance of this, a meeting was convened at which an Ambulance Committee was formed with Miss Blomfield being appointed Ambulance Officer and Percy Fisher secretary. Within a year sufficient money was raised by various events and public subscriptions to purchase an Ambulance for the town and this was delivered in March 1944.

The Red Cross instituted a Medical Loan Service for the town in 1946. By 1948 sufficient money was raised in the town to buy the first Red Cross Trailer for Norfolk. This had been specially designed by Mrs Coryn, one of the members, and her husband and was first used at Snetterton Race Track. With the help of Messrs G. Elsegood, R. Durrant, J. Kittell and A. Peeke-Vout, the Red Cross Detachment constructed a Model Hospital, fitted out in every detail and it was on display at the Royal Norfolk Show at Anmer Park in 1950 and visited by Her Majesty the Queen, who also inspected the Red Cross Trailer. Officers and members of the Detachment formed a Guard of Honour for Her Majesty and Miss Blomfield and Mrs Coryn were presented to her.

Following the disastrous floods at Cley in 1953 where the Detachment did heroic work, Miss Blomfield received a commendation from the King and also the Red Cross Badge of Honour and Life Membership. Mrs E. M. Farrell, a founder member who served as Quarter Master, secretary and treasurer until 1972 was also presented with a Certificate of Commendation. Sadly, the Red Cross Trailer was vandalised in 1976, but the Round Table kindly replaced it with a fully equipped caravan and Mrs Sadd, the Commandant, was presented with the key for it the same year. In 1980 Mrs Rachel Sadd received the Red Cross Badge of Honour and Life Membership for her long and devoted service, over 40 years. Mrs Mary Riches, who was assistant Commandant until 1984 was presented with a Certificate of Commendation the same year. The present Commandant is Mrs Irene Parrott and Mrs Sadd is now the Centre Organiser.

*Watton Detachment of the Red Cross, No. 42. Miss Blomfield, the Commandant, is second from the left and Mrs R. Sadd on the extreme right of the front row.*

# ST. JOHN AMBULANCE BRIGADE

Before the last war Sir Thomas Cook, the County Commissioner of S.J.A.B., purchased the disused Wesleyan Chapel for the use of a Division in Watton, if and when, one could be formed. An attempt by two people just before the war, and another attempt just after, were unsuccessful.

In February 1949 Mr C. M. Dupont who had been taking the Association Examinations in Surrey for 20 years, came to live in Watton. Three months later his record card was transferred to Norfolk and when Sir Thomas received this he arranged to meet him. The outcome of the meeting was that Sir Thomas asked Mr Dupont if he would try to form a Division in the town.

After meeting Miss K. Blomfield, the Commandant of the Red Cross Detachment, who promised to do everything she could to help, he was successful in finding eleven other men, who together with himself attended a course of First Aid Lectures in the autumn of 1949. Dr R. G. Shanks was the lecturer and the Red Cross Society loaned bandages, splints and other equipment until St. John's had enough funds to purchase their own. All twelve men passed their examinations and Mr Dupont was appointed Divisional Officer (later Divisional Superintendent) and Dr Shanks Divisional Surgeon. A year later an Ambulance Cadet Division was formed with 18 boys and Mr H. J. Rump the Headmaster of the school was appointed their President.

When Mr Dupont and Mr Rump left the town in 1952 Mr J. H. Page of Carbrooke was appointed Divisional Superintendent of the Watton Division and Mr R. Waters became Divisional Officer in charge of the Cadets.

For a while, during the 1940's, the old Chapel was used as a Health Clinic and during the early part of the 1950's it was hired by the Norfolk Education Committee for three nights a week as a Youth Centre where table tennis, snooker and billiards were among the amenities provided. By the mid 1950's the old building was deteriorating badly and under the leadership of J. H. Page, the divisional Superintendent, sufficient money was raised and with financial help from Sir Thomas Cook, it was demolished in 1958 and the present St. John's Hall erected on the site. This was officially opened in the spring of 1959. In addition to the main hall, there is a Dr's consulting room and a kitchen. The present Divisional Officer is David Skipper of Ashill.

*Opening of St. John's Hall by Lord Walsingham in 1959.*
*Left to right: Victor Woods, Arthur Kerridge, Ronnie Waters, Tony Sussams,*
*Roy Banham, Philip George, Dr. Puddy, John Riley, Lady Cook, Sister Mollie*
*Lambert, Lord Walsingham, Arthur Neve, Sir Thomas Cook, Martin Dupont,*
*Rev. Avery, Mr W Crawford (President), Harry Page, Dr. G. R. Shanks, Bob Moore,*
*Stanley Clarke, Ted Houchin.*

# THE CARE OF THE ELDERLY

The first batch of Grouped Home bungalows in Lime Tree Walk were occupied in May 1963 when Mrs Sara Farrall, the first Warden, and her husband John moved into the centrally situated Warden's House. Adjoining that is the large Communal Room where the residents of the 20 two-bedroom bungalows could meet for a chat, play games, hold their Christmas Party and enjoy a variety of other entertainments. In 1972 a further 12 single-bedroom bungalows were built alongside Church Walk and are also in the care of the Warden.

A few years later another 18 two-bedroom bungalows were added in Lime Tree Walk for elderly residents who were well enough to look after themselves and therefore do not come under the care of the Warden. These were occupied in October 1976 and two years ago they were connected to a new Alarm System whereby they could summon help in an emergency. Few residents over the age of 80 will equal the feat of Mrs Alderton, who lived with and cared for her mother, Mrs Fanny Jolly who died in her 105th year. On her 100th Birthday, and four more after, she was visited by council officials and Mr and Mrs Sample, the florists, presented her with a bouquet of flowers for five years after reaching her century. Lindon Court, set in pleasant surroundings on the opposite side of Church Walk, was opened in 1966 as a home for 45 elderly people. A new extension was added in 1983 for a further 16 residents and opened just before Christmas. This comprised four blocks of 4 self-contained flats, each with a comfortable and well equipped bedroom, a communal dining-living room and fitted kitchens, complete with fridge and cooker rings. It is the latest concept in the care of Norfolk's elderly of having their own homes within a home. Here they can choose their own level of independence. They don't have to do anything if they don't wish too, but if they feel like it, they can keep their rooms spic and span and maintain their independence. They are also at liberty to join in with the other residents in the main lounges and take part in all the home's activities.

*Lindon Court, a home for the elderly, in Church Walk. March 31st 1985.*

115

# CHANGES ALONG THE HIGH STREET

Standing in front of Julnes's China Shop on the South side of High Street offers a clear view of the property on the opposite side from the West End Stores to the Dereham Road corner. To one who has known this view for well over sixty years, two contrasting things immediately come to mind. First, if we look towards the skyline we still see much the same miscellaneous assortment of roof tops of a century ago, with their various shapes and sizes giving them a charming, even if somewhat, higgledy-piggledy appearance. The few high level changes along this stretch during my lifetime can almost be counted on one hand. George Elsegood's house replaced two old thatched cottages in 1953 and two years ago Ling's extensive motor cycle shop replaced the area where Bob Kittle's cycle shop, and adjoining house and the long demolished Chequer's Inn once stood.

Next to the Brewery two shops with flats above were erected about thirty years ago and a little further along Barclay's modern bank now stands on the site of the once popular "Green Man" Inn. Next door, Jack Cross built a new cycle shop in 1937, but the tiles weathered so well that within a few years the casual observer would not have noticed any difference. A re-tiling job was carried out on Edward's a few years ago and here again the weathering effect was so good that it hasn't affected the character of the roofs on this side of the street. Lastly, we come to the corner of the Market Place where George Butcher's ironmonger's shop had deteriorated over many years, especially when it stood empty for so long following Hubert Amy's time, that there was only one thing for it. It was demolished in 1978 and Roy Rudling's imposing D.I.Y. store erected to give this area a state of respectability once again. Now let's take a look along the same stretch at ground floor level when we will immediately notice a vast contrast during the last sixty years, or even the last ten. Apart from the long established family business of Sharman's and four private houses west of Ling's, I don't think there is another property that has not changed and many of them quite extensively.

What has happened to the majority is that originally they had a shop at the front with a larger area of living quarters behind. Many of them have had the interior walls of the living accommodation removed and the ceilings reinforced to create an extensive shopping area, which in some cases now runs almost through to Harvey Street. The private houses that intersected the shops in my youth have now been converted into shops offering a wide variety of goods. Recently Adcock's have not only extended their own T.V. and watchmarker's shop, but have also acquired what was once Vincent's Chemist Shop.

*High Street, Watton early 1900s.*

*A.T. Edward's Shop 1925. Left to right: F. Dalton, F. Edwards and O. Fincham.*

*Watton Post Office Staff and Postmen circa 1912.*
*Third from left is W. Lyles, 4th A. Bailey, 6th J. Whalebelly. Mrs Stibbon, the*
*Postmistress is in the doorway with her husband on her right. Next but one is*
*postman Brown and next to the elderly man is Tom Drew.*

These two shops, with the living accommodation and storage areas behind them, have now been converted into one large shopping area by joining up behind the old Clock Tower and incorporating the "Pop Inn" record specialists under the same roof. From here to the pathway through to Harvey Street, Sharman's is the only business still selling the same commodity as they did in my school days, long may they continue. Curtis's sports shop was then Hilton's boot and shoe shop and three sisters, Helen, Maud and Emma Pearson had their wool and fancy draper's shop where the Peterborough Building Society now operate. McEwen and Green's – later MacLaren's – ladies and gents outfitters, is now the Spar Grocery Shop. Carter's large furniture store occupies the premises where Chaston's harness maker's and Smith's barber's shop were. The Post Office has been on the same site for nearly a century. In my young days it was a small sub post office only, but now it is also a stationery and book shop as it was in William Stace's time, over eighty years ago. One of the oldest properties in High Street was Edmund Adcock's watchmakers, now a goldsmiths and jewellers and it dates back to at least 1710 and is probably much older.

*Ernest Adcock outside his shop in the late 1920s*

Next door, Julnes's pet and seed shop has been extensively modernised. From here to Clarence House, only one shop is still in the same business as when I passed it on my way to school. Then it was John Bullen's butchers, later William Stebbing's, then Riches Bros., and now Doubleday's. Even Clarence House, the most imposing house in the High Street, was converted into a shop a few years ago. Arthur Snare's private house and the office he used in his capacity of Registrar of Births and Deaths, is now a Cafe. From the old National School – now Grahamme Woodyatt's Fabrics Centre – to the Thetford Road corner few new buildings have been built on the south side of the street the last sixty years. In fact until the new International Stores and King's Chemist's was opened on September 11th 1984, I can recall only four new building sites along this stretch. Lloyd's Bank now stands on the site of the famous "George Hotel" and a hairdressing salon with flats above was built next to Julnes about twenty-five years ago. The meadow where part of the Wayland Show used to be held now accommodates the Police Station, Dr's Surgery and the Library. For the first time in living memory there is now a shop in Beechwood Avenue, Studio Khyber's Photographers.

*William Stebbings outside his Butcher's Shop 1935. It's now Doubleday's.*

*H. Reeve's Saddlery and Harness Shop circa 1916.*

By far the largest development in the High Street during the last century has seen the demolition of Codling's shoe shop, formerly the Liberal Club and Holmes's garage showrooms, to make way for King's Chemist shop and the new International Stores, part of which stands on the ground of the Liberal Club Bowling Green. Three new shops are about to be opened on what was Holmes's bottling stores. The front garden of another of the town's finest houses, "The Gables", is now the site of "Bounty Electrical". The prominent corner shop that was Harry Reeve's saddlers and harness makers business is now Dean's Estate Agents, and on the opposite side Collin's Chemist shop is now "The World of William Brown".

*The "George" Commercial Hotel circa 1885.*

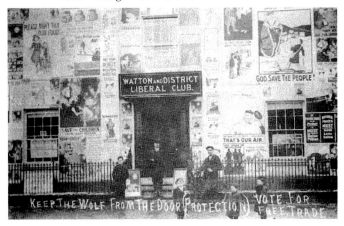

*The Liberal Club covered with Election Posters about 1913.*

# CHANGES AROUND THE TOWN

At the junction of Harvey Street and Dereham Road, where the first International Stores in the town was burnt down circa 1915, one will find the East Anglian Insurance Brokers. The King's Arms in Middle Street was demolished and rebuilt in 1923 when Ted Lovewell was the landlord and Brian and Sally Worby have had a new 30 seater restaurant added which was opened on April 5th 1984.

One of the largest business developments in the town is on the corner of Norwich Road and Church Road. Frank Dye started his motor business in 1920 in a small garage, which is now the Stone Mason's workshop. It expanded so quickly that in the following year he moved into a large new building on the west corner of Church Road and the same year he was appointed one of Ford's Main Agents. Soon after the last war the present show rooms, workshops and main offices were erected. Following his death in 1968 the business was taken over by his sons Frank and Noel who purchased Smithson and Burroughes (formerly James Garner's) blacksmiths and engineering works in 1969. This is now the tractor display area, car body repair shop and car washing plant. The adjoining house built by "Nipper" Garrod for his family has also been purchased and converted into Offices.

When Julnes and Sons finished their grain and cattle food business a few years ago, their extensive premises on the east corner of Norwich and Church Roads were acquired and now accommodate one of the largest displays of Grade I second-hand cars in the county. In 1936 Frank Dye (Senior) was selling a new car that was claimed to be "Britain's Best Light Car", the Popular Ford Saloon, for only £100 and it cost just £6 to tax it.

On Griston Road, Direct Deliveries established a large furniture store over twenty years ago and since then a number of other commercial buildings have been erected along this road.

Mr George Barton founded the Watton Sawmills Co., circa 1913, on the Thetford Road site now occupied by the Fire Station and Malcolm Johnson's bungalow. Their brick offices still remain on the roadside adjoining the house known as "Lyndhurst" and during the 1930's these offices were used as the local Labour Exchange.

*Harvey Street about 1906.*

*The first International Stores in Watton where the East Anglian Insurance Brokers is now. 1929.*

*International Stores gutted by fire circa 1915.*

During the first war the sawmills supplied much timber to the government for use in the war effort. In 1916 Mr C. W. Turgoose joined the firm and from then on they expanded rapidly and soon after the war they had outgrown this site and moved to a much larger one next to the Railway Station. They were proud of the fact that they erected all their own large buildings on the new site to house the most up-to-date woodworking machinery, entirely with their own labour and using the best seasoned English Timber. Shortly after moving to the new site Mr Barton left the firm and Mr Turgoose and Mr Soper became the directors and from then it became the Wayland Timber and Sawmills Co. Ltd. They claimed to be able to supply anything connected with the timber trade and also manufactured fowl houses, garages and sheds of every description. At this time they were by far the biggest employers of labour in the district. In 1929 it was sold to a Yorkshire firm and a few years after that was closed down. By 1935 the site was taken over by H. Bardwell and Sons, Timber and Builders' Merchants. Today George Tufts and Son Ltd. are carrying on in much the same lines, but have greatly extended their range.

In the early 1870's Horatio Goodrick had a thriving business on the Thetford Road corner. He was an iron and brass founder and agricultural implement maker and many of the old "built in the wall ovens" that were the only means of baking at this time, were made by Horatio, and later by his son Nehemiah, who finished his working life at James Garner's engineering works in Norwich Road. These premises were converted into a motor garage in the early 1920's for Ridout and Lovewell. Later H. J. Ridout, who over the years built up a large business and was the sole agent for Standard Cars, also supplied Triumph and Vauxhall cars and Bedford lorries. After six years on the Dereham Road corner, where Dean's is now, John's Discount Stores moved into John Ridout's former garage which enabled them to spread their wings four-fold. Their short move was undertaken in February 1977.

Just after the war the building firm of Day and Nowak Ltd., came into being, which was started by two ex-servicemen in an old barn behind Whalebelly's butchers shop, now Fennell's. In 1952 the firm moved into their own premises when they converted the former butcher's slaughterhouse into an office and workshop and created a builders yard at the rear of the building, the entrance to which was off the Thetford Road. During the next 33 years their developments included the buildings of Charles Avenue, Churchill Close and Nelson Court estates with some smaller developments and private houses in Watton and the surrounding district.

*Dye's Garage 1928.*
*Left to right: F. Ward, F. Dye, P. Button, J. Roberts, C. Tyrrell, – – – and J. Gant.*

At their peak some 50 houses a year were built, employing 90 to 100 workmen. To cope with the extra business the firm leased the former builders yard and offices of Waters and Sons until 1963 when they purchased eight old cottages on the Thetford Road and converted them into the builders offices and the extensive Hardware and General Stores (J.P.N. & Co. Ltd.).

About eight years later this business was further expanded when they purchased the former Bull Hotel Bowling Green, which now accommodates their wide range of building and gardening requisites. During the late 1930's Mr.E. Madoc founded the Bee Apiaries on what old Wattonians called "Crab Tree Corner". Soon after the last war the modern honey processing building was erected and Miss Jessie Roberts, another well known beekeeper, went into partnership with him until they both retired.

In 1961 Ted Savoury started his architectural design consultancy firm of Edward A. Savory and Associates. As the business expanded he decided to start building houses as well as designing them. In 1967 he formed Modus Developments and one of the first residential sites they built was in the grounds of the former Cottage Hospital. The hospital itself was converted into temporary offices until they moved to the former honey processing factory at the junction of the Thetford and Thompson Roads in 1972. These premises were greatly extended and converted into modern offices and given the name of 'Barn Ruche'.

The first big step in the firm's growth was the building of the Vicarage Walk estate of nearly 300 homes. Other sites built by the firm included Garden Close, Wick Farm and over 100 homes at Lovell Gardens. In the council housing sector Modus built 65 homes for the Breckland District Council at Stokes's Avenue 20 weeks ahead of schedule, realising a significant saving to the council in interest terms. At this period the firm were the largest employers of labour in the town.

Another of their ventures was the building of 15 Unit Factories on the site of the former Railway Station. These were opened by Mr. John Hill, then M.P. for South Norfolk, in October 1973. Two of these were occupied by Modus Cars and their racing exploits have carried the name of Modus, and therefore of Watton, throughout Britain and Europe with considerable success. In 1975 they won the John Player Formula Atlantic and British Super Vee Series and were second in the B.P. Formula Three championships.

*The Watton Sawmills Co. works on the site of the present Fire Station, 1919-20.*
*Standing on extreme left with his young son is George Barton, the founder of the*
*firm. Standing in front of the timber drug is Mr C. W. Turgoose who later became the*
*managing director. Others in the picture include F. Button, F. Watson, A. Pipe, S.*
*Fickling, R. Garrod, H. Dennis, W. Disdle and A. Francis.*

In April 1976 the new Modus M/7 Formula Two Racing Car was unveiled at their Watton factory, having been built in 9 weeks.

Due to the economic climate, inflation, flatness in house sales, owing to the high cost of borrowing money, the Modus Group of companies ceased business in November 1976. Shortly after that their impressive 'Barn Ruche' headquarters were taken over by Millhouse Poultry until they also went out of business in May 1982. Three months later the Macro Group acquired the Barn Ruche complex and it was further extended to provide Industrial Units for letting. Having now centralised their building and property development group at Barn Ruche, Macro's have recently converted the old honey processing factory in the centre of the complex into a modern joinery and customised timber workshop.

The oldest business still in existence on the Brandon Road is Abbey's Engineering Works founded in 1910 by James Abbey, who in the same year built his own bungalow, believed to be the first in Watton. During the first world war the firm was making small specialised parts for use in our warships. Soon after the war they became one of the pioneers of wireless in East Anglia and manufactured thousands of aerials and other apparatus, many of which were exported all over the world. At this time they also manufactured galvanised pig and poultry troughs, tanks, barrows and water carts. These works were considerably enlarged in 1932 when they started manufacturing hand-operated petrol pumps. The Second World War saw the firm once again switch over to important government contracts to assist the war effort. Mr Abbey was also in charge of the Royal Observer Corps during the last war. To-day, the firm are still working on government contracts and also manufacturing garage equipment.

*Ridout and Lovewell's Garage about 1929. Left to right: J. Freestone, J. Ridout and B. Green.*

The extensive business of G. D. Bowes and Sons Ltd. was started in 1954 by Mr. Dudley Bowes in the former Liberal Club building in Watton High Street. Two years later the business transferred to new premises on the Brandon Road.

During the next 25 years the business expanded from killing less than 1,000 pigs per week, and selling whole pigs mainly to Smithfield Market, to killing over 6,000 pigs per week, more than half of which were cut and prepared for National supermarket chains and meat manufacturers. In the late 1970's it was decided to modernise the plant to E.E.C. Standards, enabling the company to trade worldwide. At this time the company employed a total of 280 staff on their Brandon Road premises and pig producing units.

In November 1984 a disastrous fire destroyed most of the factory, which is now being completely rebuilt. During the rebuilding programme the company will be taking advantage of the latest technology in the meat trade and this will enable them to expand their existing markets and further develop worldwide trade. The present directors are Mr Ashley Bowes, Mr. Kevin Bowes and Mrs F. M. Bowes.

*G.D. Bowes & Sons, Ltd., "Breckland Butchers",*
*complex before it was destroyed by fire.*

No mention of the new industrial estates in Watton can be made without the name of Poll Withey springing to mind. When this Double Glazing firm, who only a few years ago were making windows in an old chicken shed, decided to purchase a 3 acre site on the Threxton Industrial Estate at Watton and build a 22,000 sq. foot factory and office complex, no one could have visualised that within a year or so they would not only make themselves, but also the town of Watton, a household name all over the world.

On 20th July 1984, a whirling Red Helicopter of the Queen's Flight whisked one of their V.I.P. customers in for an hours tour of their Watton factory. Poll and Withey had recently received an order from Princess Margaret to make a dozen Double Glazed Windows for her Kensington Palace Home. After installing them they invited her to visit their new 10,000 sq. foot extension which she accepted. The Princess winced in the glass cutting room as a screeching saw set her teeth on edge, but despite this she was very impressed with the neatness of the factory and the quality of the staff. In October 1983 the firm took advantage of sponsoring Norwich City Football Club and when they won the Milk Cup Final at Wembley on March 24th 1985 the game was televised over most of the world and the name of Poll and Withey of Watton, was seen blazed across their jerseys by millions of viewers. The following evening the team and officials made a tour of the City in Abel's open-topped bus before attending a civic reception at the City Hall. This enabled millions more television viewers to see Watton well and truly put on the map by these two most enterprising Watton firms.

In contrast to Poll and Withey's large factory, there are a number of small units available to anyone starting a business, and 3 months ago the Watton Tool and Hire Centre, who started in a small shop beside the brewery two years ago, moved into one of these units. Here the father and son business is expanding so fast that they are already outgrowing their new premises and their success is sure to encourage others of the many advantages of starting a business in Watton.

Following the death of John Partridge, his house and meadows on the Dereham Road were purchased by Billy Friend and during the next twenty years he built up one of the largest scrap merchants businesses in East Anglia. Like some other businesses in the town, it became so large that he had to move to a larger site on the Griston Road industrial estate about fifteen years ago. From the time he left school, his son Paul assisted his father in running the business and upon his father's death ten years ago, Paul continued to manage it until it was sold about a year ago.

On the Dereham Road the stables and hayloft of the former 'Live and Let Live' Inn were converted into workshops by the Weatherhill Bros., David and Paul, in 1981, later to be joined by younger brother Mark. Here they make Tents, Marquees, Awnings and Covers etc., and in 1983 they won the contract to recover the whole of the Norwich Market Stalls. Over 250 were supplied in yellow, white, red, blue and orange to create a most colourful spectacle in the city centre.

*Princess Margaret, escorted by Timothy Colman, Lord Lieutenant of Norfolk, visiting Poll and Withey's factory at Watton on July 20th, 1984.*

# A FEW SCHOOLBOY MEMORIES

On my way to school from Redhill Nursery Farm, where I was born, one of the first people I saw was John Pymer, an elderly man who was the gardener at the vicarage. He would usually be standing at the entrance gate leaning on a stout stick chatting to a passer-by. It was his custom to allow himself plenty of time to get to work so that he could enjoy a little mardle with someone before starting work behind the high garden wall, as apart from the vicar, he probably would not see another person until his days work was over. He needed the stick for support, because he had the misfortune of having a wooden leg and considering this handicap, he kept the large vicarage garden in "very good trim".

My next early morning scene was often of Mr Pipe, a one-armed man, taking a timber drug hauled by a team of heavy horses through the town to collect a load of newly felled trees. He usually returned to the "woodyard" (now Tuft's) between 5 and 6 p.m. and I marvelled at the skill which enabled him to load the drug single-handed with only one hand and a metal crook in place of the other. Beside the entrance to the wood yard was Robert Davey's tobacconist and confectioners shop. He was known locally as "Doctor" Davey, because he would relieve one of an aching tooth, his small fee of one shilling however, did not guarantee a painless extraction. The smell of burning hoof still lingers in my nostrils from Garner's Blacksmith shop as Bill Crane fitted a set of new shoes on a farm horse.

*William Crane, the Blacksmith who worked for James Garner's for 57 years.*

131

Two shops that held a fascination for boys in those days were the harness makers, Reeve's (now Dean's) and Chaston's (now Carter's furniture shop). Here we watched skilled craftsmen through the windows as they made a new horse's collar, or repaired a set of old harness. Both Edward's and Harvey's newsagent shops always had a fine display of toys in their windows that attracted youthful eyes and I well remember receiving a fret-work set from one and a Mecanco set from the other, as Christmas presents.

Both bakers displayed mouth-watering goodies and Moore's, on the Dereham Road corner made the most delicious doughnuts. Graver's (now Elliotts Frozen Foods) specialised in pork pies and sausage rolls. The most popular shop with children, however, was Mrs Chamberlain's confectioners, now an insurance agents. Children crowded in here on their way to school to spend their pennies, or even a farthing, which in those days would buy a stick of liquorice. However little one had to spend, her cheery greeting was always the same, "Hullo, my little dear and what would you like today".

A penny would buy so much then, with a choice of bull's eyes, coconut crisps, gob-stoppers, hum-bugs, jelly babies and sherbert, to mention just a few of her popular lines.

Sharman's was the most popular butchers shop with the boys because the genial grandfather of the present manager kindly gave us the occasional pigs bladder which could be inflated to make an excellent substitute for a football. Wednesday was the day many boys looked forward to most and as soon as school was over they dashed up to Hall and Palmer's and Barnham's Sale Yards to earn a few coppers helping farmers to drive home their purchases of cattle or sheep. On one occasion another boy and myself drove half a dozen frisky young bullocks to a farm two miles away. Having finally delivered them safely, after a few exiting escapades over some gardens, the farmer was full of praise for our efforts, thus giving us hopes of a fair reward. He then said, "Do you boys keep rabbits?". As almost every boy of my generation did, it was no surprise to him when we said "Yes".

Pointing to a heap of swedes as large as footballs, he said, "You can have as many of them as you can carry home". We both took one under each arm, but after a quarter mile we had to leave them on the verge as our arms ached so much.

When shopping at Kendall's one day, the customer in front of me did not appear to be very bright, but informed the new assistant that she would like a score of eggs, but only if she could have all "Black Hens Eggs". In those days they were sold by the score and were not graded.

A large basketful was standing on the counter with a ticket saying, "Fresh eggs 1s. 2d. a score". Looking puzzled, the assistant remarked that he could not tell a black hen's egg from another, but told her that if she could, she could help herself. After she had gone the assistant asked me if I could tell a black hen's egg. I replied that after watching her, I could, as she had chosen the 20 largest eggs in the basket. This taught me that a person could well be brighter than appearance suggested.

Mr Knight, our schoolmaster, was a great musician and the conductor of the local Choral Society. He had no interest in any sport and we were never allowed to play football during school hours. Once a week during the summer, if no one had misbehaved, we were taken to the "playpiece" the last hour on Fridays, for cricket. It was then that the boys of my age got to know Charles Lintott, the previous head master, who was a great cricketer. Here he gave us both instruction and encouragement in the noble arts of the game. Offering 3d to any boy who hit a boundary, or took a wicket and if we could hit two sixes, or take two wickets in one over, we were rewarded with 6d, a lot of money in those hard times.

Stepping off the mid-day train on Tuesdays was the dapper figure of Mr Challis carrying two large, flat, baskets and crying his wares, "Fresh cream cheeses". Another familiar character was Bob Cockrell, who, with his pony and cart, hawked the town crying, "Live cockles, live cockles, green samphire, green samphire". Another character who was always good for a laugh was Albert Eyre, a watchmaker whose shop was next to Clarence House. Whenever he saw a few boys approaching he would roll about as if drunk. Thrusting a hand deep into – what must have been a specially made pocket – he would produce the largest pocket watch I ever saw, about 8in across and 1in thick. He would then say, "Can one of you boys tell me the time as I can't see the figures on this little old watch".

With only a few horse drawn vehicles and one or two cars, the children had the freedom of the streets and on their way to school the boys indulged in such pursuits as hoop running, top spinning, marbles and pop guns while the girls favoured hop-scotch and skipping ropes. Next to "Show Day", the most exciting day of the year for school children of my generation was Empire Day, May 24th, set aside for the celebration of the Anniversary of Queen Victoria's Birthday. On this day all school children from Watton and the surrounding villages marched through the street, headed by a band, to the meadow that is now the site of Charles Avenue, where sports were held, dancing round the Maypole and a most scrumptious tea provided. In the procession the two leaders of each school carried a Union Jack, or a banner with such words as, "One King, one Empire", or "For King and Country", emblazoned across it.

Sunday School outings were also much looked forward to and the earliest ones I remember going to were Mr Howe's Church Farm at Threxton and Mr Saunders's Broadmoor Farm at Carbrooke. Later we were taken to the seaside in a solid-tyred "Char-a-bang" and on one occasion when going to Sheringham some of us had to help the "old lady" up the hill a mile or two from Holt.

To the older residents of Watton any mention of Loch Neaton would remind them of one of its former caretakers and a true Norfolk character. For many years Sam Hose carried out his duties in a faithful manner and boys at this time who bought a season ticket to use the pleasure grounds regarded Sam as a kind inspector whose chief delight was to uphold rigidly all the regulations printed on the admission card. Usually Sam was generous in the half hour allowed for hiring a boat, but crafty boys would keep the boat well away from the mooring posts as the 30 minutes was about up. Then Sam would shout out in his rich Norfolk voice, "Come yew on in bor with that theer bote". Strangely, the young oarsmen would suddenly become remarkably hard of hearing. An up-to-date swimming pool such as is now being constructed was beyond Sam's wildest dreams. During the winter he and an assistant would go out in an old punt and cut the weeds with a scythe so that the people could swim in the natural lake the following summer.

In his early days Sam was one of the horse-drawn mail cart drivers between Shipdham and Thetford calling at Watton Post Office for the mail before continuing along the lonely 12 mile drive across the heath via Smoker's Hole and Frog's Hill, to Thetford. He was also the last landlord of the "Live and Let Live" Inn where his son "Wink" kept a horse and cart. One evening we were having tea on the day of a District Council Election when a hard knock on the door caused my father to answer it in haste. The next thing I heard was, "Hev'ya bin to wote yit guv'ner. dew I'll teark yew an tha missus in me ole hoss an cart, but don't yew forgit to wote fur tha missus, will yew". Opposite the old "Live and Let Live", where Mrs Friend now lives, John Partridge had a smoking house for curing hams. In my schooldays most people in the villages surrounding Watton kept a couple of pigs. One they would have killed for the family's use and the other was sold to pay the rent and other commitments. The hind legs of the pigs were taken to John for converting into mouth-watering hams and the front legs were usually made into pork cheeses.

*Empire Day scene on Market Place, 24th May 1907.*

*Empire Day Parade 24th May 1909, with Liberal Club in front, left.*

*Market Place, 1930s.*

# MISCELLANEOUS

When Adcock's were expanding their T.V. Shop in 1982 workmen re-discovered an old tunnel under the building which was said to be 30 feet long, seven wide and high enough for a man to stand up in. For Michael, it brought back memories when he dared his school boy friends to go into it. He also thought that it could be as old as the house, which according to a date on the wall, was built in 1674. I also think that it would have been constructed when the house was built. This is most interesting. Was the house one of those destroyed by the fire of Watton on 25th April 1674? If so, no time was lost in rebuilding it. Or was the fire in April 1673, as most old records state? However, according to one reference I have come across, 1673 was an error, as the fire was in 1674. Another question is, what was the original purpose of the tunnel? It is well known that the part running under the former chemist shop was used by Lacy Vincent and Benjamin Chaston, his predecessor, as a wine and spirit store. So could the shop and tunnel have originally been built for a wine merchant? Probably, but after reading on, you may well think this unlikely. When the new sewer was laid along the High Street in the 1950's, certain modifications had to be made to circumvent the tunnel. The man in charge of this work informs me that although the tunnel had been sealed off near the pavement, he was able to remove a little rubble and with the aid of a powerful torch could see that it went under the High Street towards the Crown Hotel. At the opposite end it had been sealed off near the end of the chemist's property, but he was able to see that this end of it went under Harvey Street, towards the house that until 1926 was the "Red Lion" Inn. This was also confirmed by a man of 88 who helped with maintenance work in the tunnel when only 14 and the older workmen told him to keep a look out for their employer coming along, as they had partaken of too much wine stored there and were going to sleep off the effects. He also stated that another branch of it went under the buildings towards Roy Rudling's Stores. I would be interested if anyone can throw more light on the subject.

*The Police Station on Thetford Road Corner 1856.*

# THE TOWN PUMP

Many are the changes that have taken place in Watton since I was a boy and although most of them have improved the character of the town, or provided it with modern amenities there is one thing I have always felt rather sad about. This was the removal of our ancient town pump situated in a place of honour in front of the clock tower. Unlike most village pumps that were operated by a long iron handle heavily weighted at the lower end, being lifted up and down, our pump was unique as it had a circular wheel with a short handle attached to it at an angle of 90 degrees. To obtain a supply of water this handle had to be rotated in a circular motion whereupon the water came out of the curved spout and into a bucket placed beneath it. Any water that overflowed was channelled down to the roadside into a drinking trough for passing cattle on their way to the market and for the tradesmen's horses. The pump was protected on three sides by sturdy oak posts and iron railings and all were demolished in the week commencing September 13th 1948. I was not alone in feeling sorry to see the old pump go as it had served both man and animal faithfully for many generations and it never failed them, even in the worst periods of drought. It was a familiar landmark in our small town and today it would have been an immense tourist attraction that could well have brought increased trade to the town. Until the town was connected to the mains supply in the 1930's most of the residents living near the town centre had to get their water from this source.

A favourite game for children was for one of them to jump onto the horizontal handle and balance himself over it on his tummy, a friend would then turn the handle at a steady speed to give him a thrilling circular ride. With the clock conveniently situated above the pump these rides were usually timed to last two minutes; then it was the turn of the next boy, or girl, as the case may have been. During these joy rides one always had to keep a sharp look out for Police Inspector Earle with his cane, but at least these escapades ensured that the cattle trough was always full.

When helping to form a barricade of sand-bags around the Police Station in September 1939, I was speaking to Police Inspector Brunson when a young sandy-haired lad of about eight went past and the Inspector had a little chat with him. Turning to me again as the lad was leaving, he asked if I knew him and I replied that I did not. The Inspector then said, "I'll tell you a little tale about him. He has not lived in Watton long, but every Wednesday lunch time you will see him at the market, taking a keen interest in all the animals". During the recent school holidays I saw him looking at the few goats for sale, so I said to him, "Do you like them sonny", whereupon he replied, "Yes, I would like to have that one", pointing to a young one. I told him that I also liked that one. An hour or so later the police station bell rang and when a constable answered it, a young lad said, "Please could I see the Inspector". When I went to the door, there stood this lad with a goat, who said, "Please sir, I have bought you the goat that you liked". Asked how much he paid for it, he replied 1/6 (7½p). Well sonny, that was good of you to buy it for me, but as I have nowhere to keep it and you also said you liked it, here's 2/6, now take it home and look after it". The Inspector went on to say, "That boy will go a long way". How right he was. Have you guessed? His name was Noel Abel.

*The most celebrated stallion in England of the 1870's, Honest Tom, bred by William Welcher, of Snare Hill, Watton, in 1865.*

Now for a story of two contrasting animals. It may not be generally known, but one of the most celebrated stallions in England was bred by William Welcher, a Watton farmer. Lancashire is justly famed for its fine shire horses, but it was a Norfolk-bred stallion, "Honest Tom", that transformed the quality of cart horses in the north-western county.

In a book published a few years ago entitled, "The Shire Horses", it was revealed how the history of the breed is inextricably interwoven with that of the county of Norfolk. But the story of how Honest Tom left his home at Watton to take the "red nose" is one of the most intriguing horse tales of all time. Bred by Mr William Welcher in 1865, Honest Tom, in five successive years—1867 to 1871 —won first prize at the Royal Show. This fine achievement made Honest Tom the target of a wealthy Preston cotton mill owner named Miller, who was determined to procure only the best, to improve the horses in the Fylde area. Miller travelled to Watton to persuade Welcher to sell Honest Tom to him. He was reputed to have come loaded with golden sovereigns which he produced in instalments until Mr Welcher's reluctance was overcome. In Lancashire, Honest Tom went on to win his sixth successive first prize at the Royal Show, this time for the Fylde Company in 1872. In the same year that Honest Tom won this latest honour, a photograph appeared in the local newspaper showing Stebbings, the Watton street cleaner – who always wore a Top Hat whilst doing his work – standing beside his donkey and cart. What a sad contrast this poor wretch must have made with the fine physique of the champion stallion. The photograph of the street cleaner was taken outside what is now Carter's furniture shop and there were no raised pavements at that time.

During Kett's Rebellion in 1549 Watton was over run by a military force of over 12,000 armed peasants during July. In the spring and summer of that year there was widespread hardship and rioting in the county. This was caused when many of the common lands were fenced in by the local gentry, thus denying the peasants their common grazing rights for their cattle and sheep which enabled them to support their families.

The peasants set about destroying the fencing and Robert Kett of Wymondham, who had visions of a better Norfolk, led the rebel movement. He made it clear that he was not rebelling against the government in London, but against the local government of the county. Thousands of peasants rallied to support him and their first military attack was repulsed at King's Lynn. Kett and his rebel army then retreated to Watton for regrouping. Here their forces rapidly increased and when nearly 20,000 strong they moved towards Norwich which they attacked on the night of July 31st.

Fred Robinson, a member of a Watton family of solicitors who practiced in the town for over 75 years, was known throughout England as an eminent Norfolk botanist. A member of the Botanical Exchange Club, he contributed no fewer than 3,700 sheets between 1913 and 1924. He discovered a number of plants around Watton that were new to Norfolk and in 1909 his was the first record for Cerastium arvense var. latifolia, in the country.

*Stebbings, the Street cleaner of Watton, always wore a "Top Hat" when he was at work. This photograph was taken in 1872, outside what is now Carter's Furniture Shop.*

*The unveiling of the War Memorial 1920. Note the "Live and Let Live" Inn sign.*

*Proclamation H.M. King George V. 20.5.1910, two bandsmen playing Bob Kittell and Tom Garner.*

One of the pleasantest walks in the town is along the avenue of Lime Trees between the War Memorial and the Church. The trees were planted by the parishioners of Watton in commemoration of the Coronation of Edward VII which took place on August 9th 1902. In the same year a pair of heavy metal gates and railings were erected at each end of Church Walk, as it became known, kindly donated by Lord Walsingham. Originally it was very muddy in the winter, but about fifty-five years ago it was asphalted at the expense of Mrs Davey, who owned a confectioners shop where the betting office is now.

Watton was cut off from the outside world by 8 feet high snowdrifts on February 25th 1958. Many children attending Swaffham Grammar School and workmen at R.A.F. Station, Marham were unable to get home, some of them for two nights. Blinding snow storms on February 15th 1979 also cut off the town and Mr. Reg Edwards of Sharman Avenue was flown to the West Norwich Hospital by helicopter for an emergency operation to save his sight.

From the early 1870's Robert Button and Sons were builders, undertakers, timber merchants, wheelwrights, carpenters, plumbers, glaziers, decorators and bridge builders with premises covering four acres in Brandon Road. They built some of the bridges still in use in the district to-day.

From about 1879 Semmence Bros. kept the Jolly Farmers Inn. William Semmence was a wood turner who had a large contract with the dye manufactures in Lancashire for making wooden bowls used in their dye works. His brother Albert was a mineral water manufacturer who moved from the "Jolly Farmers" in 1912 to a site in Cley Lane, next to the Gas Works and later moved to the "Garden House" on Norwich Road where he finished business in the late 1920's.

During the turn of the century Fred Garner had his coach works next to the railway line in Norwich Road. Here he turned out many types of horse carriages and he was also the pioneer of the motor car in Watton. His first car was an "Argyll" and it was reputed to be capable of an incredible speed of 10 mph. The lads of the day lost no time in "dubbing" it, "Bonny Mary of Argyll". Little Freddie, as he was affectionately known, was the "king of ice skating" at Loch Neaton, where he cut the most intricate figures and designs.

In May 1980 a number of empty houses on the R.A.F. Station became home for 65 Vietnamese refugees, these so-called "Boat People", who had no home or security and very little privacy for nearly five years, spent many weeks on the open seas in small boats before arriving in Watton. Many people in the town and the adjoining village of

Carbrooke had given furniture, clothing and time to help set up the rehabilitation centre and others had volunteered to befriend the families outside the camp by introducing them to life in the local community. An open day was also arranged for June 14th when residents from Watton and the nearby villages were invited to visit the camp and meet the refugees informally.

*Believed to be the first aeroplane to land in Watton when it made an emergency landing on a meadow in "Cley Lane" in 1912. It was a 60h.p. Caudron bi-plane piloted by W. H. Ewen of the "Daily Mail" aeroplane circuit.*

Watton's Evening Women's Institute was formed in 1948 and Miss Cracknell was its President, and Mrs J. Farrall the Secretary for 17 years. In November 1950 their Choir won first place for advanced Women's Choirs at the King's Lynn Musical Festival. The wooden seat outside the Post Office was presented to the town by the Institute in March 1960. An Afternoon Institute was also founded in the town in December 1976. In August 1974 Watton became one of the first towns in Norfolk to start a W.I. Market which still continues to thrive. Watton and District Silver Thread Club was formed in March 1951 by the Red Cross and St. John's with 17 members enrolling. Now there are nearly a hundred members.

When Watton's new shopping precinct in the High Street was opened in September 1984 a lead-lined time capsule was buried under the flagstones containing a glimpse of the town's past and present. A copy of the "Thetford and Watton Times" was placed in the oak casket by the editor, Mr. Barry Hartley. Also included were leaflets on the town, its council, Rotary Club, Girl Guides and a Charles and Diana Crown Coin.

When I was a boy there were 13 public houses in the town, but the Railway Tavern, Live and Let Live, Red Lion, Green Man, Chequers, Black Horse, Jolly Farmers, Carpenter's Arms and Dog and Partridge have all gone. In the last few years two new ones have opened, one at "Ye Olde Willow House" and the other at West House which was built in 1805 and was formerly the home of Mr. Blomfield, the veterinary surgeon. Rodney and Brenda Hewitt had it converted into a spacious public house and named it the "Hare and Barrell", the title being taken from the town's emblem. It was officially opened on 4th July 1977 when Mr. Roy Rudling, the Town Mayor, pulled the first pint.

*Rokeles Hall*

The Domesday Book mentions that Watton had two Manors, one of which was held in 1065 by a woman named Aldreda. In 1237 Rokele's Manor was granted to Richard de Rupella, or Rokele, and in 1249 his son William had the court here. When he died issueless, his brother John succeeded him and he granted a messuage to Richard de Wadeton, this was the rise of Watton's free tenement, which was afterwards joined to the Manor of Curson's. Richard de Wadeton was one of the Barons who stood up for their liberties against Henry III, but ultimately took the side of the King and was made Sheriff of Norfolk, and in 1266, Governor of Norwich Castle.

The original Rokeles Hall appears to have been built during the 1200's and it was rebuilt in 1653 and this date is still to be seen on the north gable, but most of the present building was erected in 1888.

*The Manor House, facing Middle Street is now a Solicitors Office.*

The Manor House, in the centre of the town, has been the home of solicitors from at least 1791 until the death of Mr. Charles Robinson. During the same period the adjoining property, which is now Peter Watt's audio and video shop, was the solicitors office. From 1949 to 1952 the Manor House was occupied by Mr. G. M. Dupont and then it once again became the home of a solicitor until Mr. Smith moved into the Manor Cottage which he had built in the same grounds. Since then the Manor House has become the solicitors offices. In 1845 W. H. Hicks Esq., was Lord of Watton Hall Manor and John Land Esq., was Lord of the Manor of Rokeles.

The buildings adjoining the car park on the Thetford Road were built circa 1875 for Samuel Short, a baker in the High Street. Here he stabled the horse and cart used for his business and also the horse trap used for pleasure. He also had a large "Baker's Oven" built in one of the buildings and this is still there. It was used when his own oven at the bakehouse had to be repaired. This operation was carried out every few years and the oven was out of commission for two or three weeks, as repairs could not be started until the oven had completely cooled down which took nearly a week. By arrangement with Mr. Short, the other bakers in the town at that time also used this oven when their own was under repair. Following Mr. Short, the business was taken over by Mr. John Moore and later by his son Donald, who still used the premises for garaging their horse and cart and later the delivery van and a car.

The Watton Town Sign, erected near the town clock, is made of bronze and recalls the legend of the "Babes in the Wood", by depicting two "babes" lying under an oak tree. It was unveiled on June 15th 1959 by two children in the annual carnival dressed as "babes". It was given to the town by the Rotary Club and formally handed over by Mr. F. J. Faulkner and received by Dr. R. D. R. Shanks, the Chairman of the Parish Council, on behalf of the Town.

After working for the Workers' Educational Association for 35 years, 30 of them as secretary of the Watton Branch, Miss Jessie Roberts was appointed President of its Norfolk Federation in 1975, an honour she richly deserved. Her work for the local branch has been particularly valuable and she has been chairman of the Eastern District for a number of years. Joining the Watton branch in 1940 when she moved to the town from Bury St. Edmunds. Only one person has been a Watton W.E.A. member longer, her great friend, Miss Nora Wace, who was a founder member in 1939.

During the past 35 years Watton has had at least four women centurions. Mrs Fanny Smith was 101 on January 2nd 1960, Mrs Elizabeth Chase was 102 on 23rd February 1965, Mrs Fanny Jolly was 104 on January 31st 1969 and Miss Louie Toombs was 100 on December 24th 1982.

Two employees of Lloyd's Bank, Lesley Allum and Alison Suthers, added a spot of glamour to the forces of Law and Order in the town when they became the firt ever women to become Special Constables at Watton in January 1980. Also for the first time in its 25 year history Watton Chamber of Trade elected a woman as Chairman in 1980, Mrs Maud Cator.

Ernie Edwards cycled the 60 miles from Hyde Park Corner to Brighton to raise money for the British Heart Foundation when 61 years of age in May 1981. In June 1984 he completed the ride for the fourth time.

Whenever old "Wattonians" speak of the Wayland Show, the name of Sydney George immediately springs to mind. For 51 years his unselfish and untiring work as the Show Secretary was in no small way responsible for its success over the years. Following his retirement as secretary he took on the less arduous position of treasurer for about twelve years, truly a remarkable record.

In 1948 the Society presented a challenge shield for annual competition to Watton Area School. It was to be called "The S.S. George Challenge Shield", and Lord Walsingham, the Show President, remarked that it would remind future generations of the years of unselfish work Sydney George had put in and something to encourage them to do likewise in their turn.

Twenty years ago the newly formed Watton and District Youth Club, supported by a Parents Committee, suggested the erection of a temporary building for the Club's activities on what is known as "The Play Piece", in Harvey Street. This led to a more ambitious scheme, the erection of a permanent building and in the spring of 1966 plans for a permanent Youth Centre was approved by the Planning Authorities. The next task was that of fund raising. It was ascertained that if £600 (a lot of money at this time) could be raised by voluntary effort towards the cost, a grant could be obtained from the Department of Education and Science, providing all the work was done by voluntary labour, with the exception of a few technical items.

Various fund raising events were organised, and with some generous donations, the money was raised and work on the site commenced with great determination. The completion of this project was entirely due to those who gave of their leisure time to build a Centre of which Watton and District could be proud. The centre was officially opened on 21st September 1968 by Dr. F. Lincoln Ralphs, the Chief Education Officer for Norfolk.

The object of the Youth Centre was to help and educate girls and boys through their leisure-time activities so as to develop their physical, mental and spiritual capacities that they may grow to full maturity as individuals and members of society and that their conditions in life may be improved.

An extension of the Sports Hall, Lobby and Gents Toilets was completed in January 1974, and an extension to the Balcony was opened on 11th January 1983.

The Youth Centre building was taken over by Norfolk County Council on 1st April 1975.

*Brian Leggett arriving at Saham Toney Church, with Bob Garner and John Adcock helping him off-load the pig he had carried 1½ miles from Watton abattoir for a £10 bet on October 4th 1959. The pig weighed 2 stone more than Brian.*

*In the Bar at the "Rose Inn", about 1886. Second from left G. Long, extreme right R. Moore.*

*"Rose Inn" completely destroyed by Fire, about 1889. It was thought a spark from the chimney set fire to the thatched roof.*

# IN CONCLUSION

Few towns the size of Watton can claim to have such a wide range of fine shops selling almost everything that one could obtain in a city and a leisurely stroll around the town would convince anyone of this. Situated on the main roads between Thetford and Dereham, Attleborough and Swaffham and 35 minutes drive to the fine city of Norwich and the historic town of King's Lynn, with the beauty and charm of the North Norfolk coast and the renowned Norfolk Broads all within 45 to 60 minutes drive. In addition, the enchanting Breckland Heaths with their unique meres are right on our doorstep. Here also are many delightful picnic sites, leading to exhilarating forest walks which are at their glorious best in autumn when the amber of maple, the lemon of popular, the flaming red of beech, together with the golden bracken, create a scene of royal splendour. Little wonder then that many people have discovered Watton the ideal place in which to live.

Besides the organisations already mentioned there are many others in the town, a number of whom have raised large sums of money to provide various amenities for the elderly and disabled, etc. They include the Rotary Club, Round Table, Inner Wheel, Ladies' Circle,

Young Farmers, British Legion, F.E.P.O.W., Chamber of Trade, Guild of Artists, Wayland Players, Army Cadets, to mention just a few.

With good communications providing easy access to the whole country, it is not surprising that Watton has attracted a number of small industrial developments that have become established on the site of the former Railway Station, Griston Road and a small part of the R.A.F. Station at the east of the town. At the opposite end, the Threxton Estate on the Brandon Road is proving immensely popular and here more space is now available for development. With plenty of high quality local labour available, it is expected that these sites will soon be taken up. Over the centuries the community spirit and determination of the people of Watton has been much in evidence as will have been noted throughout much of this book and the townspeople can feel justly proud of what they have accomplished by voluntary effort.

What is it that has enabled a small town like Watton to achieve so many ambitious programmes over the years while other places three times as large have struggled to carry out far smaller projects? The answer appears to be in the spirit and determination of a comparatively small band of townspeople whose enthusiasm and inspiration has encouraged spontaneous support and active help to be given by many.

Their motto could well be, "Work hard and play hard". A good example of this was provided by Percy Vincent, whose family kept the chemist shop next to the Clock Tower for many years. He was one of the Town's keenest sportsmen of the 1890's, before leaving his native town for London. His enthusiastic work and integrity in the City brought him many honours. Becoming Sir Percy Vincent, Bt., he was appointed a Sheriff in 1926 and Lord Mayor of London in 1935-6.